PRAISE FOR *ONBOARDING*

"A must read for anyone bringing someone new into their organization—if they are serious about setting them up for success! Well organized, easy to understand and implement."

> —Andy Kriz, Director,
> The Human Capital Institute

"This book shows you the MOST successful way to ensure new recruits deliver for you. It's filled with practical tips! Why would you settle for anything less?"

> —Robert Rigby-Hall, SVP and
> Chief Human Resources Officer,
> LexisNexis Group

"Onboarding provides a framework and tools to rapidly embrace new employees and position them for success. A must read for high-performing organizations."

> —Tom Colligan, Dean of Executive Education,
> The Wharton School, University of Pennsylvania

"This is an invaluable resource for anyone bringing new talent into an organization. The upfront thinking and easy-to-use tools are key to making any external search a success."

> —Alan Cork,
> Executive Director,
> Russell Reynolds and Associates

"PrimeGenesis has done it again. Their new book presents a completely different and clearly better way to manage the whole process of recruiting, jump-starting, and managing new employees. It's hard to imagine anyone reading this book and not deploying its tools. Don't even think about starting to recruit anyone else until you've read this book."

> —Kenneth Beck, CEO,
> CEO Connection

"This book is a must read for leaders who want to set key employees up for success and ultimately have the new employee make a major contribution to improving the outcomes of the company in half the time. I am extremely impressed by how this book gives a practical road map for ensuring that someone is ready to take a key leadership position. This is not just a book, but a great tool that I am sure I will use every time a new employee is brought onboard.

This how-to book has already helped me with our current search for a new director of development. It could not have come at a better time. After losing a key employee during poor economic times, I was concerned with how to ensure that we can transition to a new director of development and fund-raising and not lose any revenue. After reading this book, I am confident that we will be able to get the right person up and running quickly and the team will be even more productive."

—Anthony DiLauro,
MSW, President/Executive Director,
Boys Town New York

Onboarding

Onboarding

How to Get Your New Employees Up to Speed in Half the Time

GEORGE BRADT

AND

MARY VONNEGUT

WILEY

John Wiley & Sons, Inc.

CONTENTS

122824

PART III
GIVE YOUR NEW EMPLOYEE A BIG HEAD START BEFORE DAY ONE

PART IV
ENABLE AND INSPIRE YOUR NEW EMPLOYEE
TO DELIVER BETTER RESULTS FASTER

APPENDICES

P arts of this book have been around for a long time. The ideas have been implemented in the work of every manager who ever brought a new employee onboard successfully. The ideas have been obvious to anyone trying to figure out how to reduce the risk of failure of those new employees, accelerate their progress, and use the new arrival as an excuse to take the team to the next level. What we've done is take those different parts and bring them together into one cohesive whole.

We are particularly grateful to those people who have helped us pull those parts together over the past several years. We are grateful to our consulting partners in PrimeGenesis, to those who have used PrimeGenesis to help them or to help people in their organizations, and to those who support us in other ways. All share our journey of learning and discovery. All were our partners in this book, whether they knew it or not.

We are grateful to our Guest Experts. As you will see, we have different relationships with different speakers. Sometimes they spoke to us. Sometimes they wrote to us. Sometimes we repurposed what they wrote for others. Some agreed with us. Some disagreed. All helped.

Finally, we have to admit that this book wasn't actually our idea. Credit for that goes to Richard Narramore at Wiley, who inspired and enabled us to bring this spark to life.

PREPARE FOR YOUR NEW EMPLOYEE'S SUCCESS BEFORE YOU START RECRUITING

Understand the Organization-Wide Benefits of a Total Onboarding Program: An Executive Summary

A Total Onboarding Program can dramatically improve the performance, fit, and readiness for the job of every person who takes on a new role—both new hires and internal recruits. Onboarding helps to build, sustain, and perpetuate high-performing teams. More important, an organization-wide onboarding program for new employees, promotions, role shifts, and other transitions can be a culture-shaping sustainable competitive advantage.

Onboarding is the process of *acquiring, accommodating, assimilating*, and *accelerating* new team members, whether they come from outside or inside the organization. The prerequisite to successful onboarding is getting your organization *aligned* around the need and the role.

- *Align*: Make sure your organization agrees on the need for a new team member and the delineation of the role you seek to fill.
- *Acquire*: Identify, recruit, select, and get people to join the team.
- *Accommodate*: Give new team members the tools they need to do the work.

3

- *Assimilate*: Help them join with others so they can do the work together.
- *Accelerate*: Help them and their team deliver better results faster.

Effective onboarding of new team members is one of the most important contributions any hiring manager or human resources (HR) professional can make to the long-term success of his or her team or organization. Effective onboarding drives new employee productivity, accelerates delivery of results, and significantly improves talent retention. Yet few organizations manage the different pieces of onboarding well, so most people in new roles do not get clear messages about what the team and the organization wants and expects from them. Even fewer organizations use a strategic, comprehensive, integrated, and consistent approach like the one described in this book.

Why? Because onboarding is not something you do every day, it's hard to get good at it. With deliberate practice, however, you can accumulate onboarding expertise. This book shows you the way, step by step.

In our work helping organizations get new leaders up to speed quickly, we have seen repeatedly that a primary cause of misalignment and disengagement of new employees is the way that most organizations split up their recruitment, orientation, training, and management efforts. In many cases, multiple uncoordinated players oversee discrete pieces of the onboarding process and make poor handoffs across those parts. Almost everybody has a story:

- People showing up to interview candidates without a clear picture of the position they're trying to fill, let alone what strengths they're looking for.
- High-pressure interviews that turn off exactly the sort of people the organization is looking to recruit.
- Closing the sale with a candidate who turns out to be wrong for the organizational culture.
- New employees showing up for the first day—and there's no one to greet them, no place for them to sit, no tools for them to work with, and no manager around to point them in the right direction.
- New employees getting off on the wrong foot with exactly the people they need to collaborate most closely with.
- New employees left to their own devices after day one because the organization has a sink-or-swim mentality.

I have witnessed a lack of collaboration, cooperation, and coordination between the recruiting lead, the human resource generalist, and the hiring manager, that actually caused a new employee to show up for her first day on the job, without anyone knowing it. I reported to the hiring manager, and was asked to take care of "onboarding" this new employee. I was embarrassed for the company, myself, and her.

—PrimeGenesis Client[1]

A new employee's failure to deliver usually stems from one or more of four things:

1. A *role failure* due to unclear or misaligned expectations and resources (preparation miss). For example, a new global head of customer service who was hired before division heads had agreed to move customer service from their divisions to a central group.

2. A *personal failure* due to lack of strengths, motivation, or fit (recruiting/selecting miss). For example, a new head of marketing who was hired with direct marketing experience that was woefully out of date.

3. A *relationship failure* due to early missteps (head start/early days miss). For example, a new employee aggressively challenged a colleague before he or she fully understood the situation, making that colleague reluctant to share information with the new employee after that.

4. An *engagement failure* due to early days' experiences (management miss). For example, a new employee's manager who was not around during the employee's first month due to other priorities.

When any person takes on a new role, there is a risk he or she will be misaligned with the organization. When you compound this with the disruption inherent in all organizational transitions, it's no wonder so many new employees fail or decide to leave in the first six months[2] and that as many as 50 percent of new employees fail to deliver what their organizations expect.[3] Often those failures or decisions aren't apparent early on. But the seeds have sprouted, and it's very hard to change the course down the road. A new job is a turbulent event for everyone.

> *We've found that 40 percent of executives hired at the senior level are pushed out, fail or quit within 18 months. It's expensive in terms of lost revenue. It's expensive in terms of the individual's hiring. It's damaging to morale.*
> —*Kevin Kelly, CEO of executive search firm Heidrick & Struggles, discussing the firm's internal study of 20,000 searches*[4]

Consider this case. A major consumer products company was experiencing high levels of new employee failure. It turned out the organization had three distinct groups each working to improve its own area of responsibility without paying attention to the others. Talent acquisition was focused on cutting expenses by increasing the use of contract recruiters. Human resources was focused on improving the organization's orientation program. Line management was implementing performance-based compensation to keep people more focused on the most important performance-driving activities.

We helped the organization get its hiring managers more involved in recruiting and orienting new employees throughout the process. The results were immediate and meaningful. Recruiting efforts became more closely aligned with hiring managers' expectations. Selection criteria became clearer. Hiring managers took a personal interest in their new employees' orientations and related activities. Candidates and new employees felt better about the organization at every step of the way, which resulted in increases in their effectiveness over time.

Because so many people have heard (or lived) these or similar stories, many organizations are looking for solutions. Many take recruiting, interviewing, and selecting more seriously. Many have utilized onboarding software or portals to manage hiring paperwork and tasks. Many hold managers accountable for the success of their employees.

All these are good things. Do them. But you don't need this book to tell you that.

This book and its Total Onboarding Program (TOP) can take your organization to a new level of effectiveness by improving and integrating the disconnected experiences and messages new employees get during the recruiting and on-the-job learning process. This is a powerful, vulnerable time in the life of an employee. It represents the most important *teachable moment* your organization will ever have with its employees. If you can plan and get each new employee and the organization in full alignment so that intelligent onboarding becomes part of your culture, you will make a material difference in your business results over time.

We are not reinventing the wheel. Most people understand or can quickly figure out the basics of acquiring, accommodating, assimilating, and accelerating new employees. Our core premise is that things work better when all efforts point in the same direction, integrated into one Total Onboarding Program (TOP). Onboarding gets your new employees up to speed twice as fast as separate efforts to recruit, orient, and manage. It enables you to get more done in less time by:

- Compressing recruiting, hiring, and assimilation time.
- Reducing hiring mistakes by making everyone, including prospective hires, fully aware of what the job requires—from the employee and from the organization.
- Reducing new employee *buyer's remorse* and greatly improving retention.
- Aligning new employees with key business strategies.

The primary requirement is that the hiring manager lead each new employee's onboarding experience all the way through. If you are a hiring manager, start by creating the overall TOP plan (per chapter 3). Get people aligned around that plan and its importance. Take primary responsibility for its execution and coordination across people and functions as you recruit. Give your new employee a big head start, and enable and inspire them. If you are the HR manager, help your hiring managers do those things. Here's a rough chronology:

Total Onboarding Program (TOP)				
Align>	Acquire>	Accommodate>	Assimilate>	Accelerate>
		Day One	IV. Enable and Inspire	
		III. Big Head Start		
	II. Recruit			
I. Prepare				

I. *Prepare for your new employee's success before you start recruiting.* Understand the organization-wide benefits of a Total Onboarding

Program. Clarify your destination by crafting your messages to the employee and the organization, and by creating a recruiting brief. Lay out your time line, and align stakeholders.

II. *Recruit in a way that reinforces your messages about the position and the organization.* Create a powerful slate of potential candidates. Evaluate candidates against the recruiting brief while pre-selling and pre-boarding. Make the right offer, then close the right sale the right way.

III. *Give your new employee a big head start before day one.* Co-create a personal onboarding plan with your new employee. Manage the announcement to set your new employee up for success. Do what it takes to make your new employee ready, eager, and able to do real work on day one.

IV. *Enable and inspire your new employee to deliver better results faster.* Make positive first impressions both ways. Speed the development of important working relationships. Provide resources, support, and follow-through.

We created this approach out of the best of what we've seen and developed in PrimeGenesis' onboarding work since 2002 with a wide range of organizations around the world like American Express, Cadbury, Johnson & Johnson, MTV, Playtex, and others. The Total Onboarding Program has delivered breakthroughs in onboarding effectiveness and organizational success for hundreds of managers and client organizations.[5]

As you are working through the steps of onboarding, it's helpful to think about your role within the analogy of putting on a theater production in which your new employees are actors. You are:

- The *Producer:* While preparing for success and recruiting, think of yourself as the show's producer, assembling resources for the show.
- Then, the *Director:* While giving your new employees a big head start before day one, think of yourself as the show's director. You will co-create the plan, make introductions, announce the show, and generally get things ready.

• Finally, the *Stage Manager*. After your new employees walk out on stage, you will continue to Encourage—Align—Solve—End (EASE) their way by managing context and the things happening around them.

The analogy is helpful because it gets you off the new employees' stage. You can't recite their lines for them. You can't hit their marks. Your job is offstage.

The balance of this Introduction outlines the steps of a Total Onboarding Program and the remaining chapters of this book. Throughout, "Total Onboarding Program plan" and "TOP plan" refer to your plan as the hiring manager, integrating all the steps of onboarding. The "personal onboarding plan" is the plan you co-create with your new employee regarding his or her own accommodation, assimilation, and acceleration.

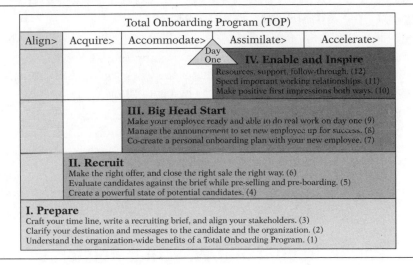

Total Onboarding Program (TOP)				
Align>	Acquire>	Accommodate>	Assimilate>	Accelerate>

IV. Enable and Inspire
Resources, support, follow-through. (12)
Speed important working relationships. (11)
Make positive first impressions both ways. (10)

III. Big Head Start
Make your employee ready and able to do real work on day one (9)
Manage the announcement to set new employee up for success. (8)
Co-create a personal onboarding plan with your new employee. (7)

II. Recruit
Make the right offer, and close the right sale the right way. (6)
Evaluate candidates against the brief while pre-selling and pre-boarding. (5)
Create a powerful state of potential candidates. (4)

I. Prepare
Craft your time line, write a recruiting brief, and align your stakeholders. (3)
Clarify your destination and messages to the candidate and the organization. (2)
Understand the organization-wide benefits of a Total Onboarding Program. (1)

Part I: Prepare for Your New Employee's Success Before You Start Recruiting

Chapter 1: Understand the Organization-Wide Benefits of a Total Onboarding Program: An Executive Summary

This chapter describes the importance of a single, integrated Total Onboarding Program and serves as an executive summary.

Chapter 2: Clarify Your Destination and Messages to the Candidate and the Organization

This is where we move from theory to practice. Start by stopping to reconfirm your organization's purpose, priorities, and desired results. How will your new employee contribute? Think through what went well and less well when you and/or your organization onboarded new employees in the past. Map out clear, simple messages about this onboarding: your message to stakeholders, your message to candidates, and your message to your new employee.

- *Manager:* Reconfirm context. Determine your messages.
- *Human Resources:* Help align messages with organization's direction.

Chapter 3: Craft Your Time Line, Write a Recruiting Brief, and Align Your Stakeholders

This chapter is about sharing your thinking with others, getting their input, and deciding together how you are going to go forward. Start by crafting an onboarding plan that includes the work you did in chapter 2, a recruiting brief, and a TOP time line. Then get important players aligned around your plan. Investment of time here makes everything else more effective and efficient down the road.

- *Manager:* Create and get alignment around your TOP.
- *Human Resources:* Help align the hiring manager's onboarding plan with the overall organizational strategy.

Part II: Recruit in a Way That Reinforces Your Messages

Chapter 4: Create a Powerful Slate of Potential Candidates

Take charge of the employee acquisition process by laying out and implementing a comprehensive marketing plan that starts with your target and moves through where you are going to fish for new employees, the tools and resources you will use, and your time lines/milestones. Communicate, demonstrate, and live your employment brand every step of the way. Assemble a deep slate of strong candidates at the same time to give you options, so that you don't feel you have to close the sale with your lead candidate if it's not 100 percent right for everyone.

- *Manager:* Inform and guide recruiting efforts.
- *Human Resources:* Manage recruiting execution. Deliver candidates that fit.

Chapter 5: Evaluate Candidates against the Recruiting Brief while Pre-Selling and Pre-Boarding

While candidates can focus on getting you to offer them a job and then take a step back to evaluate the opportunity, you must buy and sell at the same time. Make sure you are recruiting and interviewing in a way that communicates your employment brand. We use a strengths-focused, targeted selection/behavioral approach to interviewing with good success. We complete the interviewing process with formal post-interview debriefs, information gathering outside the interviews, and post-interview follow-ups with candidates to learn even more (and set up closing the sale later).

- *Manager:* Make the hiring choice—while pre-selling and pre-boarding.
- *Human Resources:* Manage the interview process. Provide a broader organizational perspective.

Chapter 6: Make the Right Offer, and Close the Right Sale the Right Way

You know your organization is awesome. Just remember that a potential new employee may need to be convinced. So treat the offer as just one part of a strategic sale. The way you handle this and support your offeree's due diligence efforts will impact the way he or she feels about you and your organization, with implications far beyond whether the answer is yes or no. You want offerees to say "yes" if taking the job is the right move for them, their supporters, and the organization over time. You want a "no, thanks" if it's not.

- *Manager:* Close the sale. Support your new employee's due diligence efforts.

- *Employee:* Do a real due diligence.
- *Human Resources:* Support manager by preparing offer and supporting strategic selling efforts.

Part III: Give Your New Employee a Big Head Start Before Day One

Chapter 7: Co-Create a Personal Onboarding Plan with Your New Employee

Co-creating a personal onboarding plan is the beginning of your working relationship. Listen, and demonstrate how much you value your new employee. Work together to think through the job and its deliverables, stakeholders, message, pre-start, and day one plans as well as personal and office setup needs. Clarify who is doing what next.

- *Manager:* Co-create new employee personal onboarding plan.
- *Employee:* Co-create personal onboarding plan.
- *Human Resources:* Provide tools and support.

Chapter 8: Manage the Announcement to Set Your New Employee Up for Success

Making the announcement is one of the most important things you can do to help make your new employee feel welcome, valued by, and valuable to an organization he or she can take pride in. Think through and implement these steps:

1. Map the stakeholders (chapter 7).
2. Clarify the messages (chapters 2, and 7).
3. Lock in the timing and wording of the official announcement.
4. Map out whom to talk to before the announcement, when and how.
5. Map out whom to talk to after the announcement, but before the new employee starts.
6. Implement, track, and adjust as appropriate.

- *Manager:* Clarify and deliver messages. Set up new employee's pre-boarding conversations.
- *Employee:* Conduct appropriate pre-boarding conversations with stakeholders.
- *Human Resources:* Manage implementation of announcement.

Chapter 9: Do What It Takes to Make Your New Employee Ready, Eager, and Able to Do Real Work on Day One

1. Accommodate work needs (desk, phone, computer, ID, payroll, forms, etc.).
2. Accommodate personal needs (family move, housing, schools, etc.).

Mind the details to give the new employee a first day that is in line with the opportunity/shared purpose and to put your new employee in a position to do real work starting day one.

- *Manager:* Ensure your organization produces a perfect day one.
- *Employee:* Clarify your needs and expectations. Get a head start on personal setup.
- *Human Resources:* Manage implementation of accommodation activities.

Part IV: Enable and Inspire Your New Employee to Deliver Better Results Faster

Chapter 10: Make Positive First Impressions Both Ways

Everything communicates. Pay attention to what people hear, see, and believe. Pay attention to the impact the organization is making on the new employee. Pay attention to the impact the new employee is making on the organization. Design the day one experience as you would a customer experience. Don't leave first impressions to chance, because while people don't always remember what others did or said, they always remember how they felt.

- *Manager:* Manage first impressions. Welcome. Introduce the new employee.
- *Employee:* Manage first impressions.
- *Human Resources:* Manage implementation of day one plan.

Chapter 11: Speed Development of Important Working Relationships

Assimilation is a big deal. Doing it well makes things far easier. Getting it wrong triggers relationship risks. There are a couple of things beyond basic orientation that can make a huge difference. We suggest you set up onboarding conversations for your new employee with members of his or her formal and informal/shadow networks. Do periodic check-ins with those networks. If there are issues, you want to know about them early, so you can help your new employee adjust.

- *Manager:* Facilitate new employee assimilation initiatives. Be alert to challenges.
- *Employee:* Invest in assimilating into the formal and informal networks.
- *Human Resources:* Support. Coach new employee and manager. Provide required resources.

Chapter 12: Provide Resources, Support, and Follow-Through

The first step in giving your new employee the resources and support he or she needs is confirming your own requirement and appetite for change. If all you need is for your new employees to assimilate into the existing culture, you can probably mentor them yourself or with an internal coach. However, if achieving the desired results requires a new employee to assimilate into and transform the team at the same time, you will need to bring in external assistance. (If insiders could transform your culture, they would have done so already.)

Make sure your new employee garners needed resources and establishes the building blocks of a high-performing team, as appropriate to his or her position:

1. What most needs to be accomplished (in place by day 30).
2. Clarity around what's getting done, when, by whom (by day 45).

3. One or two strongly symbolic early wins (identified by day 60, delivered by month six).

4. The right people in the right roles with the right support (by day 70).

5. A communication plan implemented on an ongoing basis.[6]

- *Manager:* Support. Mentor. EASE: Encourage—Align—Solve—End.

- *Employee:* Build the team. Deliver results.

- *Human Resources:* Support. Coach new employee and manager. Provide required resources.

Follow Through

Just as onboarding starts long before day one, it ends long after the personal onboarding plan is executed. Follow through with your new employee to ensure ongoing adjustments and success or to redirect if things are not working. And check the process: audit, adjust, and plan improvements in anticipation of the next onboarding.

How to Use This Book

This is very much a how-to book, designed to be used instead of read. The Total Onboarding Program is your framework—the starting point for effective onboarding. But you may also want to drill down in specific areas like recruiting and interviewing, and to take advantage of the many practical worksheets and resources in the book.

Each Chapter

- *Ends with a summary and recommended actions:* You may find it useful to look at the end of chapter summary before you read the chapter in depth.

- *Contains forms and tools:* Many of them are filled out as examples in the text. Many are downloadable from www.onboarding-tools.com as Word documents so you can fill them in for your situation.

- *Includes a Master Class callout just before the chapter summary:* These provide ways to take your organizational knowledge and skills to the next level. They're pulled together into an organizational transformation approach in appendix I.

As much as possible, we tried to avoid jargon or consultant speak. Where we felt compelled to use special words, we included them in the glossary at the end of the book.

How you handle the acquisition, accommodation, assimilation, and acceleration of new employees communicates volumes to everyone. In many ways, this is one of the acid tests of leadership. If you follow the prescriptions in this book and stay focused on inspiring and enabling others to do their absolute best together to realize a meaningful and rewarding shared purpose, then those others will happily follow you.

CHAPTER 2

Clarify Your Destination and Messages to the Candidate and the Organization

Prepare

Total Onboarding Program (TOP)				
Align>	Acquire>	Accommodate>	Assimilate>	Accelerate>

Day One IV. Enable and Inspire

III. Big Head Start

II. Recruit

I. Prepare
Craft your time line, write a recruiting brief, and align your stakeholders. (3)
Clarify your destination and messages to the candidate and the organization. (2)
Understand the organization-wide benefits of a Total Onboarding Program. (1)

Don't begin to recruit anyone until you understand how their role is going to help deliver results that move the organization forward in line with its purpose and priorities.

Now What?

He had been a standout star in everything he'd done from high school through college through his early jobs. Every single person HR and the hiring manager talked to during reference and background checks had nothing but positive things to say about him. They were all thrilled to have been able to convince him to join the firm.

Now what?

No one had fully expected him to say yes.

No one was exactly sure what his responsibilities should really be.

Now it was time to figure that out.

Now was way too late.[1]

Start by Stopping

Onboarding begins with your business objectives. Start by stopping to figure out what you want to accomplish and how you expect your future new employee to deliver or contribute to target results. Think business strategy. You risk leaving a lot on the table if you treat hiring as a transactional event as opposed to a strategic opportunity:

- *"Just fill the position."* Hang on. Will the position as defined deliver the results you need? If not, this is a great time to recraft the job to further your business strategy.
- *"Find me the best candidate."* The best at what, precisely? Do you need the best skill set, or will the individual's inherent behaviors and motivators be more important to delivery of business results than skills and experience? Complete your thinking before implementing anything, even a broad search initiative.
- *"I know what I need."* You may know what you need, but do you know what your stakeholders and the new employees' stakeholders need? Without stakeholder alignment you will never make the right hire, because your new employee (no matter how great he or she is) will be burdened with incompatible expectations.

Strong execution always begins with thorough preparation. If your organization has a professional HR function, you probably have a search, recruiting, and hiring process. You may even have some kind of onboarding program. More likely than not, you don't have a Total Onboarding Program (TOP) that maximizes delivery of business results.

In this chapter, you take ownership of your new employee's onboarding and lead with your business point of view. By confirming a shared vision and making sure the role for which you are onboarding is understood and broadly accepted, you are setting up team success.

GUEST EXPERT

Andy Kriz on Comprehensive Onboarding[2]

Andy Kriz, director of the Human Capital Institute's Talent Leadership Community, is a big proponent of talent as an investment. He's convinced that where the head of human resources is not considered a key player by the senior management team—you will likely find human resources serving primarily an administrative resourcing function. Conversely, where there's a human resource department that views people as one of the most important drivers of organizational success and takes a real Talent Leadership approach to their human capital—you find the head of human resources viewed as an integral part of the senior management team with titles such as chief talent officer.

The latter are the human resource professionals who think well beyond onboarding as a transactional event to onboarding as an essential part of the overall talent leadership process. Often seen merely as a process to assimilate new hires, onboarding can be used as a tool for knowledge transfer, engagement, retention, and development—accelerating performance and driving results. Too often, onboarding looks like this:

Welcome New Leader! Here's your office—I'll let you get settled in and come back to take you to lunch to talk about how you are going to take us to the next level in the marketplace and what you have done with the rest of this morning to get us there.

If you haven't experienced this sentiment yet—brace yourself!

A comprehensive approach to onboarding is essential to setting new leaders up for success. It is this critical aspect of change management that is too often overlooked or undersupported. Companies known for talent development have CEOs and leadership teams that make talent a top priority. Managers at all levels are accountable for creating a work climate that motivates employees to perform at their best. Leadership teams receive special training to help them work together more effectively. A great leadership team ensures that the investment in development results in the right number of people, of the right quality, ready when the organization needs them now and in the future. This is why comprehensive onboarding is so important.

First, Your Destination

Begin with your organization's general purpose and main priorities. That's the big picture destination. Next, drill down to the specific destination for this onboarding. When you onboard a new employee, you are implementing a strategy to achieve business objectives. Treat your new employee onboarding as you would any other investment. Define your business objective—are you hiring to replace? To change culture? To add capabilities? What is your expected return on investment? How will you measure your return? Use Tool 2.1 Purpose and Priorities[3] to delineate the specific results you want from your new employee onboarding.

Organizational Purpose

The parent organization's shared purpose, its reason to exist, or ultimate mission is its organizational purpose. Everything else nests within this. ("Provide life-sustaining sustenance" [food] in the example that follows.)

Departmental Purpose

The departmental purpose explains why the department exists. Departmental purpose nests within the organization's purpose ("acquire resources required to process food" in tool 2.1).

Desired Results

- Department priorities in pursuit of the purpose. Consider business, capability, and organizational priorities.
- Department plans for each priority.
- Target return and measures for each plan.
- This onboarding's target contribution.

It's important to look at desired results in terms of capability and organizational priorities, as well as business priorities. Capability priorities are human, operational, and financial capabilities you need to acquire or build. Organizational priorities are things you need to accomplish to improve your organizational effectiveness.

Just to underline the point. There's no question about the value of setting performance expectations and clarifying job scope. Some argue that hiring managers should share those expectations and guidelines with new employees during the new employee's first weeks on the job. We think

Tool 2.1

Purpose and Priorities (Downloadable)

Organization Purpose: *Provide life-sustaining sustenance (food)*

Department Purpose: *Acquire the resources required to process food*

Department Priorities, Plans:

Business Priorities	Plans	Target Return, Measures	This Onboarding
1 *Purchase vegetables*	1A *Identify appropriate veggies*		
	1B *Negotiate contracts for veggies*		
	1C *Manage supplier relationships*		
2 *Secure water supply*	2A *Strengthen water transportation system*		*Yes*
	2B *Reduce water transportation accidents*		*Yes*
	2C *Manage water transportation process*		*Yes*
3 *Purchase packaging*	3A *Identify suppliers*		
	3B *Negotiate contracts*		
	3C *Manage supplier relationships*		

Capabilities Priorities	Plans		
4. *Rain water and own crop harvesting*	4A *Hire skills*		*Partly (water)*

Organizational Priorities	Plans		
5. *Professionalize*	5A *Increase team to 30% with top engineering degrees*		*Yes*

that is way too late. Instead, job scope expectations and guidelines should be part of every step of the onboarding process so new employees completely understand them by their first day on the job.

TOOLS

The downloadable tools at www.onboarding-tools.com are an integral part of this book. They're all printed in the book itself, usually filled out as examples. We've premised the example tools on one story, to make it easier for you to see the links. The tools are filled in from the point of view of Goodfood Food Processing's head of product supply, Anna, who works through acquiring, accommodating, assimilating, and accelerating a new employee.

Goodfood is a midsize food processor that acquires resources (Product Supply—Anna's group), processes and packages foods (Operations), sells and markets (Marketing and Sales), and ships foods to retailers (Distribution).

TIME SAVER

This is one of those pause-to-accelerate moments. It may seem that taking the time to go back over the organization's purpose and priorities is a waste of time. It's not. It's a major time-saver down the road, because it provides the ultimate end point for everything you do, keeping you—and everyone else—on track.

Examine What You've Done Before So You Can Do Better This Time

When you begin each new employee onboarding with an evaluation of past onboardings, you make continuous improvement to your standard operating procedure. Use Tool 2.2 Onboarding Track Record to examine your organization's track record and your personal past successes and shortcomings—with internal transfers, promotions, and people brought in from outside the department, country, or organization. Incorporate your learning into your current plan.

Tool 2.2
Onboarding Track Record
(Downloadable)

+ Include these successes in your TOP. - Avoid these mistakes. What can you do better this time?

Step	+ Successes	- Opportunities for Improvement
1. Understand how onboarding can take the organization to next level	*Individual components OK*	*Have not linked well in the past*
2. Clarify how the new employee will meet needs	*Have recruited for specific needs*	
3. Align stakeholders' expectations of the new employee		*Have not done in the past*
4. Create a powerful slate of potential candidates	*Did good job of finding a diverse set of candidates*	
5. Evaluate candidates against the recruiting brief		*Need to make sure everyone is evaluating consistently*
6. Make the offer and close the sale in a way that reinforces your leadership message	*Have done a good job closing sales*	*Pay more attention to leadership message*
7. Co-create a personal onboarding plan with each new employee		*Not done in the past*
8. Manage the announcement cascade to set the new employee up for success	*Generally get announcement out in advance*	*Pay more attention to what happens before and after announcement*
9. Do what is required for the new employee to be ready, eager, and able to do real work on day one	*Basics generally in place*	*Should get specific tools in place for each individual*
10. Manage first impressions both ways	*Have done good job finding people that fit culture*	*Can brief new employees on what to wear, say, do*
11. Create conditions for new employees to work well early on with those who were most helpful	*Generally everyone gets along*	*Can do better job introducing new employees to peers*

(continued)

Tool 2.2 (continued)
Onboarding Track Record (Downloadable)

12. Give your new employee the resources and support they need to deliver better results faster	*Generally hire people that get up to speed quickly*	*Should reinforce new safety standards*
13. Follow through to ensure ongoing adjustment and success		*Need ongoing follow-up plan*
Other		

The tool is relatively simple:

- *Note things that went well:* Be sure to include those successes in your TOP.

- *Note things that did not go well:* Think about what you can do differently to improve the next onboarding. Think about how well you aligned your organization before you started onboarding. Think about each stage of the onboarding process: alignment, acquisition, accommodation, assimilation, and acceleration.

NOTE TO HR

Human Resources can help here by routinely conducting new employee fresh-eyes surveys. Provide the results to all hiring managers. There's more on this in Appendix I.

Stop—Do Not Pass Go Without Clear Messaging

Organizations and hiring managers communicate with candidates more than they realize during recruiting, interviewing, and every subsequent step of onboarding. Intentional and inadvertent actions and inactions leave candidates with strong impressions. Equip yourself and others to execute consistently and on message with organizational realities *at all times* by completing Tool 2.3 Messages.

Do not communicate about any aspect of your job opening until you have a set of messages and communication points with which your stakeholders are aligned. Include vetting discussions with your HR, corporate communication, and marketing partners, so that your messages coordinate with the employment brand you are building (see chapter 4). Add your new employee's message after you co-create the Personal Onboarding Plan (chapter 7). At each change, review your message for consistency across organization, department, hiring manager, and new employee. This simple tool guarantees unified messaging and a foundation for cultural integrity, up and down, inside and out.

Your messages are source material for your job announcement and all other onboarding communications. When you write your messages, be realistic about your organization. Communicate objectively, in a way that will ring true with an external observer's findings. You will not win if your new employee finds the company to be something other than what was portrayed in the ramp up to day one. Prospective candidates assess you as much as you assess them. You try to determine if the candidate is aligned with your organization's core values and beliefs. The candidate tries to determine if your organization fits with his or her core values and beliefs. Your messaging should anticipate the signs and symbols

Tool 2.3

Messages (Downloadable)

	Organization (Employer Brand)	Department	Hiring Manager	New Employee (Chapter 7)
	Goodfood Food Processing	Product supply	Anna	Sr. Associate Director Aquatic Delivery
Mission and Purpose	Provide life-sustaining sustenance (food)	Acquire resources required to process food	Acquire resources required to process food	Secure water supply
Vision	Ecofriendly company that does important work			
Values and Beliefs	—Individuality			
	—Continual learning			
	—Fun			
Message	Ecofriendly company that does important work	Department does important work	Do important work	
Signs	Interview setup procedure? Interview guidelines		Partnership approach to Total Onboarding	
Symbols	Office environment	Group camaraderie	Encouragement of group camaraderie	
Stories	Helped community during last year's flood	All pitched in to support family of injured team member	Helped injured team member's family personally	
Keywords or phrases (top 3)	Do good for others, do good	Do good for others, do good	Do good for others, the	

	for the environment, continual learning	for the organization, continual learning	environment, learn
Questions, Answers			

candidates would read to assess your organization. Test all of your onboarding documentation and communication—words, actions, signs and symbols—against your messages before release or execution.

Use your messages to prepare answers to questions candidates might ask:

- What words or phrases describe the organization's culture?
- How does the company handle conflict/differing opinions?
- How does the company recognize employee accomplishments?
- Does the company have a code of ethics?
- What's the leadership or managerial style at your company?
- What qualities do the most successful employees possess?
- Are there professional and educational advancement opportunities?

TIME-SAVER

Clarity of communication saves time.
    Clarity of messaging leads to clarity of communication.
    Need we say more?

MASTER CLASS

Take this to the next level by looking at overall organizational messaging on an annual basis as part of your normal succession planning and talent management processes. Get all employees aligned around the overall messaging that they will cascade down in their own Total Onboarding Programs. This annual messaging review (1) increases consistency across individual messages and (2) gives everyone a chance for deliberate practice to build knowledge and skills in crafting and critiquing messaging.

Summary and Indicated Actions

Onboarding is a strategic exercise in that it's about building capabilities and capacity for the future. Thus, you can't begin to recruit anyone until you understand how their role is going to help deliver results that move the organization forward in line with its purpose and priorities:

1. Start by clarifying purpose and priorities.
2. Look back at your onboarding track record to make sure you keep the things that worked before and improve areas that can be improved.
3. Lay out your messages so everyone understands purpose, priorities, responsibilities, required strengths, and the most important organizational values.

Focus

- *Manager:* Look at context again and determine your messages.
- *Human Resources:* Help align messages with organization's direction.

CHAPTER 3

Craft Your Time Line, Write a Recruiting Brief, and Align Your Stakeholders

Prepare

Total Onboarding Program (TOP)				
Align>	Acquire>	Accommodate>	Assimilate>	Accelerate>
			Day One	IV. Enable and Inspire
		III. Big Head Start		
	II. Recruit			
I. Prepare Craft your time line, write a recruiting brief, and align your stakeholders. (3) Clarify your destination and messages to the candidate and the organization. (2) Understand the organization-wide benefits of a Total Onboarding Program. (1)				

Unclear or misaligned expectations and resources are some of the main causes of new employee failure to deliver.

Plan Part A: Frame a Total Onboarding Program Time Line

To make onboarding run like clockwork for your prospects, candidates, recruiting partners, and the people in your organization, frame your process with a detailed time line. Time lines eliminate most of the inefficiencies and communications blunders that delay or prevent your getting the best new employees and bringing them up to speed quickly. The idea is to think through your whole plan in advance, document it, and get alignment around it from everyone involved in onboarding your new employee. Create a time line for each individual you onboard. You will slow the whole process if you attempt to batch or cohort groups of people.

We reference the time line frequently. Keep yours at hand while you work through onboarding. Tool 3.1 Total Onboarding Program Time Line coordinates with the chapters in this book. We recommend optimum timing and accountability for each action item, but you should customize your time line for your own onboarding situation. Recruiting and onboarding more senior leaders may take longer than indicated by our starting time line. Conversely, you may be able to shorten your time line substantially when recruiting and onboarding junior people.

Tool 3.1

Total Onboarding Program Time Line (Downloadable)

Activity	Tool	Timing	Date	Responsibility
Complete planning tools				
—Purpose and Priorities	2.1			Anna (boss)
—Onboarding Track Record	2.2			Anna
—Messages	2.3			Anna
—TOP Time Line	3.1			Anna
—Recruiting Brief	3.2			Anna
—Employment Brand	4.1			Anna
Stakeholders aligned			4/30	Anna
Recruiter selected			4/30	Hal (HR)
		Go Live		
Recruiter briefed/ job posted		D1–8 wks	5/1	Hal
Candidates sourced	4.2		5/2-5/27	Recruiter
Candidates presented	4.3	D1–5 wks	5/27	Recruiter
Initial interviews complete	5.1,2,3	D1–4 wks	6/3	Hal
Final interviews complete	5.1,2,3	D1–3 wks	6/10	Hal

Post interview follow-ups	5.4		6/11-16	Hal
Selection made		D1–2 wks	6/17	Anna
Offer extended		D1–2 wks	6/17	Anna
Follow-up campaign	6.1		6/18-23	Anna
Offer accepted		D1–1 wks	6/24	Anna
Job plan pre-work			6/24	Anna
Job plan meeting	7.1		6/25	Anna, New employee
Job plan hand off			6/25	New employee
New employee announced	8.1	D1–4 days	6/26	Hal
New employee accommodations	9.1	Pre-Day One	6/30	Anna
New employee welcomed	10.1	Through D1	7/1	Anna
Day One				
Assimilation efforts	11.1	D1 and on	7/1 –	Anna, et al.
100-Day actions	12.1	D1–100	7/1-10/10	New employee
Feedback		Week 1		Anna
		Day 30		
		Day 60		
		Day 100		
		Month 6		

Some parts of our time line may be different from what you are used to. Refer to Tool 3.1 as we walk you through the timing and rationale for each step. We'll describe the details of each step in subsequent chapters of this book.

Time Line Action Items

1. Plan Ready
Craft your basic plan—composed of these completed tools—before you even think about seeking the alignment you need to trigger the start of recruiting:

Tool 3.1: Total Onboarding Program Time Line

Tool 3.2: Recruiting Brief (incorporates thinking from Tool 2.1: Purpose and Priorities, Tool 2.2: Onboarding Track Record, Tool 2.3: Messages, and Tool 4.1: Employment Brand)

2. Stakeholders Aligned Around Your Plan, the Time Line, and Recruiting Brief

It is so easy to say, but so hard to do, and so important to do correctly before you implement anything. Do not delegate any aspect of gaining alignment. Communicating directly with all your stakeholders to make sure everyone sees things the same way is a pivot point of onboarding. Take your time, and do this well.

3. Recruiter Selected

By "recruiter," we mean the person who's going to assemble the slate of candidates. It could be you. It could be an in-house recruiter. It could be an external recruiter. We'll talk about the different types of recruiters later. The point for now is to select an approach.

Now you are ready to *go live* with your efforts to acquire talent!

4. Recruiter Briefed/Job Posted

If you've done a good job on the recruiting brief, this piece should be relatively straightforward. You may want to do this personally to make sure the recruiter understands all the nuances of your brief.

5. Candidates Sourced

This is the piece that will vary the most, depending on the level for which you are recruiting. Senior people take longer; junior people take less time.

We recommend you do your sourcing in parallel. Find all the best candidates internally and externally at the same time, then screen down to a manageable number for your initial interviews. Sequential job searches tend to stretch out over time and are often marked by starts, stops, and restarts. You will do a better job of keeping everyone's attention, if you do your sourcing once.

6. Candidates Presented

Have your recruiter(s) present all candidates who cleared the initial screening at the same time, so that you can compare the full universe to decide which candidates to interview.

7. Initial Interviews Complete

Some people prefer to do all the initial interviews on one day. Some people prefer to spread interviews out over several days. Doing all interviews on one day makes it easy to block out interviewers' time and allows you to compare the candidates while they are all fresh in the minds of the interviewers. Spreading interviews over several days makes it easier to preserve confidentiality. Either way, you should complete your initial interviews during a relatively short time period so that you can move on to final interviews.

8. Final Interviews Complete

Complete these as soon as practical after the initial interviews to minimize the chances of losing one of your finalists to another opportunity.

9. Post-Interview Follow-Ups

This one's a little counterintuitive and involves extra work. We suggest you take some time between the final interviews and extending an offer to perform reference checks, background checks, and to ask any follow-up questions you may have for the final candidates. Taking a little extra time here can make a big difference.

10. Selection Made and Offer Extended

11. Follow-Up Campaign

There's a lot in here. Allow at least a week to move from offer to acceptance.

12. Offer Accepted

Do allow at least a week to move from offer to acceptance; but don't allow much more than that. Every day that goes by is going to make it that much harder to convert your second-choice candidate if your first choice turns you down.

13. Personal Onboarding Plan Pre-work

Give your new employee the prework for your personal onboarding plan meeting as soon as possible after he or she accepts your offer.

14. Personal Onboarding Plan Meeting

Hold this critical meeting to create the new employee's personal onboarding plan as soon as the day after you have an accepted offer.

15. Personal Onboarding Plan Handoff

The personal onboarding plan meeting between you and your new employee is another pivot point in onboarding. It's when you move from being the one in charge of onboarding to the one supporting the new employee, who is in charge from now on. Of course you will still have things you need to do (think back to the theater production analogy in chapter 1—in this meeting you move from director to stage manager), but your new employee is now center stage, leading the efforts.

16. New Employee Announced

This should happen as soon as practical in advance of a new employee joining from outside. Coordinate the announcement with all parties involved and/or affected when you bring on a new team member from inside the organization.

17. New Employee Accommodations

As soon as you announce your new employee's impending arrival, you can get moving on setting everything up for your new employee to be able to do real work on the first day.

18. New Employee Welcomed

As we'll talk about in a chapter 10, the welcome is a big deal and powerfully symbolic. Invest time in planning day one in detail.

Now you are ready for day one!

19. Assimilation Efforts

Assimilation efforts kick in on day one and flow until the new employee is completely joined up.

20. Personal Onboarding Plan—Key Events

Plan to give your new employee extra help and support over his or her first 100 days—at least.

21. Feedback

Be diligent about gathering regular feedback to create opportunity to reinforce engagement and be alert to problems that need to be corrected.

> *No matter how long thoughtful onboarding may take, it is time well spent. Having the team together from the start, avoiding the*

complications inherent in distrust and ignorance of the "new guy" makes success far more likely. Take the time. Get the process off to a good start.

—PrimeGenesis Client

HOT TIP

Think through and get your colleagues' alignment to the components and approach captured in the Time Line before you do anything else. This is the key to guiding your implementation of discrete efforts as a comprehensive, integrated program.

TIME-SAVER

Standard operating procedure would have you believe that you can't control the time as tightly as we suggest. The argument is that some things (like sourcing candidates) take more time than you expect.

Don't buy it.

Map out your time line. Get people (including outside recruiters) aligned behind it and committed to scope, timing, and resources. Hold them accountable.

Mapping out your Total Onboarding Program (TOP) plan has a double benefit: The explicit integration will make you more effective. The tight time line and resource plan, agreed to up front, will make you more efficient.

Plan Part B: Put the Wheels in Motion with Your Recruiting Brief

Part of Lena's job was to recruit salespeople. Her district had 30 sales representatives and needed to add seven to eight new ones per year. One or two got promoted, and six or seven left for greener pastures. Her district manager prided himself on the quality of his people and wanted to make sure that all the people Lena recruited had the strengths and motivation to do a job at least two levels beyond sales representative at some point in their careers.

There was flaw in the approach. And Lena saw it.

Hiring sales representatives to become sales managers of one sort or another had the benefit of creating a strong slate of people for possible promotions. It had the downside of creating a relatively large pool of disappointed people. The math didn't work. If you hire seven to eight people a year and promote only one or two, most of the people you hire are not going to get promoted.

Someone told Lena that you can only *accept* the job offered, not the job promised. She thought that was true and decided it made sense to *recruit* for the job offered, not the job promised.

She went to the district manager and proposed a new recruiting approach: Recruit half the people to join as sales representatives with the potential to become sales managers. Recruit the other half of the people to be sales representatives. These would be people with strengths and the motivation to be great sales representatives. The district manager agreed to give it a try.

Along came Phil. Phil was a career sales representative. He was smart, affable, loved interacting with people, and loved selling, but his real passion was music. He played guitar at night—sometimes in clubs, mostly at home. He knew he was probably never going to earn enough from his music alone to support himself. So he split his life, selling during the day and playing during the evenings. He never wanted to be a manager. The extra work would interfere with his music. But he had had a long and successful career in sales.

Hiring Phil (and others like Phil) changed the dynamics of the district over the next few years. Every year, three or four new people were brought in who competed for the management promotions. Half got them, and half left. And every year, two or three people were brought in as career salespeople. The benefits were significant:

- *Turnover decreased.* The career salespeople didn't leave when someone else got promoted because they never wanted promotions for themselves.
- *Number of hires decreased.* It decreased because turnover decreased.

- *Management candidates were happier.* There were fewer candidates competing for the management promotions.
- *People got excited about selling.* The new people like Phil had an infectious enthusiasm for selling. They were constantly looking for new ways to serve their customers. And they were delighted to share those ideas with others because they weren't competing for promotions.

The moral of this story is that you should think through all the reasons you are hiring somebody, carefully considering his or her impact on others in the organization, including those that you might not think would be impacted.

Tool 3.2 Recruiting Brief is the document that will drive recruiting activities from now until your ideal candidate has accepted your offer. Take your time. Do this well. Make sure your recruiting brief gives everyone involved the information and perspective he or she needs to do a superlative job.

We will reference the recruiting brief frequently. Keep yours at hand while you work through this book.

Dina hired a recruiter to find a head of information technology for the private company she owned. Here's how the process went:

- The first round of candidates didn't have enough experience.
- The next set earned too much money.
- The next group wanted equity.
- The final pool was fine, but not what the board was looking for.
- Then the chief operating officer recommended a friend who was hired.
- That person quit after three months.
- Then they went back to one of the candidates from the second set and offered her the job at a higher salary.
- But by then she had another offer.

In retrospect, they all agreed that the process would have been more efficient and effective if all parties, including the board, had agreed on the requisite experience, compensation, and other criteria in advance.

Tool 3.2
Recruiting Brief (Downloadable)

Recruit for Job Title, Department, Compensation Grade, and Start Date:
Senior Associate Director of Aquatic Delivery, Product Supply, Grade H$_2$O, to start 7/1

Mission/Responsibilities	
Why position exists	*Secure water supply*
Objectives/goals/outcomes	*Water delivered to operations on timely, safe basis*
Impact on the rest of the organization	*Operations cannot do their job without water delivered at right time and right place*
Specific responsibilities	*Manage all aspects of water sourcing and delivery*
Organizational relationships and interdependencies	*Must deal with external suppliers and coordinate with internal customers (operations)*
Vision (picture of success)	*Timely, complete, safe delivery of water to operations*
Strengths	
Talents	*Achiever, discipline, focus, responsibility, self-assurance*
Skills	*Practiced water resource manager*
Knowledge	*Physics expert*
Motivation	
How activities fit with person's likes/dislikes/ideal job criteria	*Likes working in pairs*
How to progress toward long-term goal	*Potential future director of product supply*
Fit	
Values	*Doing good for others, the environment*
Workstyle, characteristics	*Highly social group (to a fault)*
Companies	*Hands off (to a fault)*
Groups	*Attached—Purpose and Priorities (2.1),*
Supervisor	*Messages (2.3), Total Onboarding Time Line (3.1)*

This form may be downloaded from www.onboarding-tools.com, customized and reproduced for personal use and for small-scale consulting and training (not to exceed 100 copies per page, per year). Further use requires permission.

Recruiting Brief Components

Job Title, Department, Compensation Grade, and Target Start Date
Grade is code for total compensation range. It's extremely helpful to know what you are planning to pay your new employee. There are

different components of compensation falling into buckets of short-term compensation (salary, commissions, overtime, and benefits), midterm compensation (annual bonuses), and long-term compensation (deferred bonuses, retirement plans, and equity). If grade doesn't specify those automatically, spell them out. You don't want to recruit a group of people looking for high salaries and equity for a job that pays minimum wage—and vice versa.

Mission/Responsibilities

- *Why the position exists.* The main long-term responsibility and how it contributes to the organization's broader purpose.
- *Objectives/goals/outcomes.* Things you need delivered over the near term.
- *Impact on the rest of the organization.* SIPOC is a good tool to think this through. All work is a process. Processes have suppliers that provide inputs and customers who use outputs. The impact piece is how this position's outputs enable customers to do their work.
- *Specific responsibilities.* This relates to the job activities that are needed.
- *Organizational relationships and interdependencies.* This involves the suppliers and inputs part of SIPOC in terms of those who supply hard outputs and softer outputs like information and guidance (as well as links with customers because things often go both ways).

SIPOC

Supplier → Input → Process → Output → Customer

Vision

The vision is the picture of success. It's 24 months after your new employee's hire date. He has done more than you ever thought possible. You take him to dinner to congratulate him. "What a great job you've done. Everyone is so pleased with _____ ." (Fill in the blank to create your vision.)

Strengths

This is the heart of what you will recruit for:

- *Talents.* Pull from the Gallup Strengths list in chapter 5. It's not clear whether talent is innate or irrelevant. But you might as well err on the side of safety and recruit for it.[1]
- *Skills.* These are going to be some of the easiest to screen for. Skills are developed through practice over time. Spell out the technical, interpersonal, and business skills that someone needs to be able to do the job you are recruiting for.
- *Knowledge.* These are things learned. Spell out the education, training, experience, and qualifications that someone needs to be able to do the job you are recruiting for.

Motivation

- *How activities fit with person's likes/dislikes/ideal job criteria.* This pertains to short-term enjoyment of the work itself. In general, happier people perform better. Spell out criteria that should make your ideal candidate happy.
- *How to progress toward long-term goals.* This relates to longer-term things. Some people may be willing to invest in their own future and do things that are less enjoyable over the short term, if they lead to good things down the road. Detail where this position could lead with an eye toward the skills and knowledge someone can develop and acquire in the position.

Fit

On the one hand, fit is hard to gauge. On the other hand, it's crucial. Well worth specifying some criteria for thinking about how candidates might fit with the overall organization's values, and with working styles and characteristics at the company, group, and supervisor level. If one of your personal pet peeves is punctuality, don't hire the people who show up 15 minutes late for the interview without an explanation. Either they will make your life miserable or you will make their life miserable or both.

TIME-SAVER

Though it's not quite standard operating procedure, many people start recruiting without a recruiting brief or with just a general brief, planning to evolve their thinking along the way.

This is like starting to build a house without a blueprint.

Take the time to create a specific brief. It will help your recruiters find you the right candidates and weed out the wrong ones. It will help you and your colleagues do a better job of evaluating people. It will help candidates understand how they fit in the organization.

It is a *big* mistake to wing it without a recruiting brief.

Align Your Stakeholders Around Your Total Onboarding Plan

Alignment is key to successful onboarding. Thinking and planning are only the first steps. Until you have stakeholders up, down, and across the organization aligned around the role and interdependencies, you don't have an onboarding plan.

Aligning Partners

Anil decided to centralize customer service. Large global clients were demanding it. So Anil hired a global head of customer service and charged that person with creating the role in partnership with the division presidents.

The problem was that the division presidents all thought customers were their primary responsibility and were very happy managing customer service on a divisional basis themselves. So it wasn't surprising that the new global head of customer service encountered some resistance.

Ideally, Anil should have gotten the division presidents aligned around a common definition of the new role before starting the recruitment process. Then the division presidents could have become partners in making the new employee successful instead of resisters.

Clear potential obstacles to onboarding progress and your new employee's success by making sure your stakeholders are aligned around what you want and how you plan to get it. Review your destination (Tool 2.1 Purpose and Priorities), messages (Tool 2.3 Messages), time line (Tool 3.1 Total Onboarding Program Time line), and recruiting brief (Tool 3.2 Recruiting Brief) with your stakeholders. If necessary, revise your plans to improve alignment. Take note of potential problems, and use every decision point in the onboarding process as an opportunity to improve alignment around purpose, priorities, and people.

TIME-SAVER

This is another idea that improves effectiveness and efficiency. Getting people aligned around these tools can improve your thinking and execution and prevent major disasters down the road that could cause you to have to start the whole Total Onboarding Program over again. And it will make every step of the program that much easier and timely.

MASTER CLASS

Take this to the next level by embedding Total Onboarding Programs in your normal succession planning and talent management processes. As you examine what roles you need to fill in the future, get everyone aligned around hypothetical Total Onboarding Programs for those positions to give your managers a head start on filling those positions when the time is right and give everyone a chance for deliberate practice to build knowledge and skills in crafting and critiquing Total Onboarding Programs and recruiting briefs.

Summary and Indicated Actions

It is hard to overestimate the value of a well-thought-through recruiting brief and Time Line—and of getting important players aligned around them in advance. The recruiting brief guides all-important recruiting activities. Aligning others around the TOP time line dramatically increases the chances of things happening with the right sequence and timing rather than haphazardly:

1. Frame your Time Line so everyone knows what steps to hit along the way.
2. Get stakeholders aligned around the recruiting brief.

Focus

- *Manager.* Create and get alignment to the Plan.
- *Human Resources.* Help align the TOP plan with the organization's overall strategy.

PART II

RECRUIT IN A WAY THAT REINFORCES YOUR MESSAGES

CHAPTER 4

Create a Powerful Slate of Potential Candidates

Recruit

Total Onboarding Program (TOP)				
Align>	Acquire>	Accommodate>	Assimilate>	Accelerate>
			Day One	IV. Enable and Inspire
		III. Big Head Start		
	II. Recruit Make the right offer, and close the right sale the right way. (6) Evaluate candidates against the brief while pre-selling and pre-boarding. (5) Create a powerful state of potential candidates. (4)			
I. Prepare				

Having a powerful slate of potential candidates relieves you from feeling you have to close the sale with your lead candidate when a nagging voice is telling you something is not 100 percent right.

The Value of a Slate

Bert and Victor both bought fast-food franchises on the same day. Each was going to take eight weeks to close the deal and take over his store. Each needed a store manager.

Bert knew exactly the right person and contacted her immediately. She was interested. Over the next six weeks, Bert and his new store manager had a series of increasingly productive conversations about what they had in mind for the store, how the manager would be compensated, and life in general. Things went well.

Victor did not have the right person in mind, so he embarked on a full-fledged recruiting campaign. He contacted people who knew people. He placed ads. He did preliminary interviews. Two weeks before he took over the store, he was down to three good candidates.

Both Bert and Victor formally offered their chosen candidates the new store managers' jobs two weeks before opening. Both people they offered the jobs to turned them down. Bert's person had enjoyed the conversations, but because there was a delay, she used the time to find another job offer, which she decided was better for her because she didn't have to move. Victor's person decided he didn't like fast food.

Victor immediately offered the job to his second-choice candidate, who accepted and was in place on opening day, while Bert had to start the process of creating a slate of candidates while managing the store himself.

HURDLE

New to Hiring

- **Problem:** New to hiring or never been trained or need a refresher.

- **Solution:** The war for talent is real. So it is important for you to develop your candidate sourcing skills. Here is where you start:

  1. Market before you buy to attract a diverse slate of people.

  2. Start with a recruiting brief to guide everyone's efforts.

  3. Utilize a comprehensive, wide-ranging prospecting campaign.

  4. Market directly to known top performers over time.

  5. Have a simple prequalifying system in place.

  6. Hit your time lines by parallel processing the best candidates.

To put together a powerful slate of potential candidates, you need to attract and engage a large number of highly qualified prospects from which to cull your slate. The days of posting a job opening and then taking your time to select the chosen few to whom you will grant an interview are over. The Web facilitates open access to top performers. Just search profiles, publications, and events. Top performers can't hide.

The most sought after attract a lot of attention and, as a consequence, will probably not be delighted by yet another recruiting call. Public access to job openings on the Web and digital resumes also make it easy for job hunters to take a shotgun approach. If you post a job that invites nonspecialist response, you will be swamped, particularly during times when jobs are harder to find. You can set HR or a third-party service provider up as a gatekeeper to qualify prospects for you, but that can be cumbersome, expensive, and take way too much time. It also makes you, the hiring manager, further removed from the recruitment process. So despite the agility of modern communication, recruiting a powerful slate of candidates can be harder than ever.

Now for the good news—there is another approach. If you design your candidate prospecting campaign to attract and engage highly targeted prospects, you will have a smaller, better-qualified pool to work through. By keeping the process structured, fast, and efficient, you can maximize your choices and create leverage in offer negotiations by attracting good prospects, qualifying them, and engaging the ones you want to convert into candidates before any are able to slip away to competitive opportunities.

In Part I of this book you figured out and specified what you are looking for in a candidate. Your recruiting brief starts to pay off now. In this chapter, we help you develop actionable ideas about attracting the right kinds of people and how to figure out where to seek prospects, on what time line, and with what tools.

You Know What You Need, Right?

Your recruiting brief describes the candidate you think will deliver your destination business results. Precise and transparent portrayal of the job, organization, and candidate qualifications in the recruiting brief lays the groundwork for attracting motivated top performers who know what they want and who can realistically self-evaluate fit. They will be people who want a position that lets them focus on real, meaningful work.

The more your applicants are able to accurately self-qualify, the more efficient your hiring process will be. Where generalities or purportedly open-ended opportunities invite people who are unsure of what they need and want, opportunity specifics attract focus. You will get your new employees up to speed faster when you and they are as clear sighted as possible.

Revisit your recruiting brief. Make sure it is detailed, specific, and fully supported by your stakeholders. If it is inadequate in any way, stop and correct it before you start creating your powerful slate.

Market Before You Buy

Putting together your powerful slate of candidates is a marketing effort before it is a selection process. Younger workers and people in high demand look carefully at recruiting approaches when they evaluate potential employers. To compete for the best, you must offer an employment brand that excites prospects. Invest in creative ways to brand your team and company as a great place to work. Commit to the detailed planning and execution it takes to realize a successful marketing campaign. Make sure every potential prospect touch point in your organization knows and is prepared to execute your Total Onboarding Plan.

When the opportunity is communicated and candidates start to check you out, what will they discover? Can you do anything right now to make sure they find you attractive? The more appealing and widely known your organization and its *employment brand*, the more great candidates will stay in the game and the more unidentified top prospects will come forward. In today's connected world, people seek information on their own terms. Think of your efforts to put together a powerful slate of potential candidates as a two-way street. With your marketing department and human resources partners, build the best employment brand you can.

A word of warning: it is not easy to control your brand. With social networking, for example, job seekers can find—in minutes—everyone they know or ever knew who works at a company. That company's brand is on the open market, established by what those people have to say about their personal employment experiences. Make this your hiring mantra: employer brand building begins at home.

Understand that monitoring your reputation on the Web is now mandatory. Find someone in your organization to be responsible for online organization brand management. Online includes internal networks where your organization's employees collaborate and communicate. Internal forums are extremely influential to individuals evaluating internal promotion or transfer opportunities. Don't put your head in the sand.

What are people saying about your employment brand on the Web? Monitor your brand with these free tools:

- *Technorati:* The largest blog post search engine (www.technorati.com).

  Action: Comment on blog posts that mention your organization, and be sure to include hyperlinks back to your site.

- *Twitter:* The rapid-fire microblogging service (www.search.twitter.com).

  Action: When your organization comes up in a search, be sure to tweet back immediately. Your best chance to influence is getting into the conversation.

- *Google Alerts:* E-mail updates about the latest Google results based on your query (keywords, www.google.com/alerts/).

  Action: Subscribe to alerts via e-mail or RSS feeds. A great way to keep current with your competitors.

- *Backtype:* The blog comment search engine (www.backtype.com).

  Action: Track posts with Technorati; track comments with Backtype.

Corporate Rating Sites

- Vault
- JobVent
- Jobster (vertical search engine)
- Jobbite.com
- CorporateGrade.com

Tool 4.1

Employment Brand (Downloadable)

Description

We are an ecofriendly company that does important work. Our culture values expression of individuality, continual learning, and fun.

Proof

We do not harm the environment in any way.

We do good for others by providing life-sustaining sustenance to the world.

People can dress any way they'd like.

Everyone has opportunities to enroll in continuing education.

We have recreation time every day from 2-3 PM.

Brand Communication

Placement	Message	Creative
	Word of Mouth	
(Actions to influence)		
	Web Sites	
Organization sites Facebook pages	*A day in the life of your job video tour*	
	Blogoshpere	
(List important blogs)		
	Networking	
Facebook groups LinkedIn groups MySpace groups Other		
	Press Coverage/Relationships	
(List)		
	Business/Community Partnerships	
(List)		
	Advertising	
	Company Marketing Collateral	

LIFE AT GOOGLE

Google is not a conventional company, and we don't intend to become one. True, we share attributes with the world's most successful organizations—a focus on innovation and smart business practices comes to mind—but even as we continue to grow, we're committed to retaining a small-company feel. At Google, we know that every employee has something important to say, and that every employee is integral to our success. We provide individually tailored compensation packages that can be comprised of competitive salary, bonus, and equity components, along with the opportunity to earn further financial bonuses and rewards.

Google has offices around the globe, from Bangalore to Zurich, but regardless of where we are, we nurture an invigorating, positive environment by hiring talented, local people who share our commitment to creating search perfection and want to have a great time doing it. Googlers thrive in small, focused teams and high-energy environments, believe in the ability of technology to change the world, and are as passionate about their lives as they are about their work. (www.google.com/support/jobs/)

Tool 4.1 Employment Brand helps you think through your employment brand communication points. Your target is all existing employees and potential employees, and your frame of reference is employment. The *description* articulates the main benefit to an employee of working in your organization. What is particularly meaningful and rewarding about what you do and how you do it? In our example, the primary benefit is being an ecofriendly company that does important work. Cultural values of expressing individuality, continual learning, and fun are called out as well. *Proof* supports why people should believe the description. For proof to be persuasive, it must be able to be validated by people external to the organization. *Brand communication* spells out actions you will take to communicate your employment brand and notes placement, messaging, and creative choices.

Employment Branding Done Well

• AT&T (www.att.jobs/)

(continued)

(*continued*)

- Best Western (http://www.bestwestern.com/careers/index.asp)
- Starbucks (http://www.starbucks.com/aboutus/jobcenter.asp)
- Home Depot (https://careers.homedepot.com/cg/)
- Southwest (www.southwest.com/careers/)

Increasing Value

Javier used the employment brand concept in recruiting people into his group from within the company. His concept was simply that he wanted his group to be the group that:

- Everyone wants to join
- Everyone wants to recruit people from
- No one wants to leave because they know every day they spend in the group makes them more valuable

TIME-SAVER

Investing in your employment brand saves time because it makes you more attractive to the types of candidates you want to attract. Some will find you on their own after they discover a consistent, attractive employer brand in the course of networking. Others will be more receptive to your opportunities for the same reasons.

Be Cognizant of the Fit

At each decision point in the process of creating your slate of candidates, consider the importance of a good cultural fit between prospect and prospective employer. Working in an organization where the values are inconsistent with your own can be very stressful, deflating, and certainly not conducive to engagement. Don't burden your new employees with cultural fit hurdles because you relegated cultural fit to a secondary consideration when you put your slate together. If anything, cultural fit might trump skill and/or experience fit, because you can develop employee skills post-hire, but you will be hard pressed to change core values and beliefs.

> *Employees are most motivated by emotional commitment—a sense*
> *of connection to an organization's culture and purpose.*
>
> —*PrimeGenesis Client*

GUEST EXPERT

Bill Berman on the Importance of Cultural Fit in Hiring[1]

Every company and every team has a culture. Organizational culture is the set of implicit or explicit rules and guidelines that explain how you should behave, communicate, and interact within the company and with customers, suppliers, and stakeholders. Hiring people who do not have a good cultural fit can create endless difficulties, and make even the most technically capable hires struggle to succeed.

In order to pick people who fit with the organizational culture, it is essential that you be able to describe what that culture is. If you can't identify your own culture, you won't be able to tell if someone will fit in that culture. Make sure, when you define the culture, you aren't describing what it *should be*—describe what it *is*. A few key questions to ask yourself about your organization include:

- *What is the real expectation for work hours and availability at your company?* Everyone says they respect work/life balance, but companies vary dramatically in how late people work, whether they answer e-mails in the evening, and when they take phone calls.

- *How formal/informal is your organization?* I have worked with several hedge funds, none of which had more than 200 employees. Yet some expect all employees to wear business formal, and others are comfortable with jeans and polo shirts.

- *How collaborative is your organization?* Do different business functions work together to reach conclusions, or does each function operate independently? Do the regions work together, or does each regional head control

(continued)

(continued)

his or her profit and loss? How matrixed is your organization? The more matrixed it is, the more you need people who can lead by influence and shared purpose rather than driving individual results.

• *How flexible can you be in your company?* Some businesses insist that their people do whatever it takes to get the job done, and others have clear processes and systems, and want their staff to follow those explicitly. Highly flexible people will struggle with an organization that is process-driven, and process-driven individuals will flounder in highly flexible companies.

If you have trouble defining your own culture, there are lots of tests on the market that can help you describe the culture. Better yet, sit down with your team, and ask them to write single-word adjectives on 3 × 5 cards that describe the organization as it is, and as they would like it to be. Then take the cards and define your culture.

Once you know your culture, make sure your recruitment process examines individuals' style and cultural preferences as well as their skill level. Aside from the few critical skills that are essential to the job on entry, people with a good cultural fit will learn and adapt to the new role better than people with values and expectations that differ from your organization's.

When you put together your prospect candidate campaign, test every message and channel decision against cultural fit. Keep it simple. Just chart messages and channels on a skill match/culture match grid. Messages and channels that have a high match for skills and a high match for culture are, obviously, your best bets.

	Low Culture Match	High Culture Match
High Skill Match	Tempting could yield people who do more harm than good	Best
Low Skill Match	Worst	Easy to overlook could yield people who can grow into job

How Will You Communicate the Opportunity?

Perhaps your recruiter will take charge of communicating the job opening; perhaps you will divvy up the work. Do define the universe of distribution opportunities from which to choose. Include: listing openings on your organization Web sites (general site, career site, intranets), posting announcements on job boards, blogging about openings, networking, and making outbound information calls. You may want to version communications for niche groups of prospects. A word of warning: younger workers are inclined to ask "what's in it for me?" at each stage of onboarding. Assume they can and will evaluate every opportunity with a degree of cynicism.

Messages for Different Generations

- **Traditionalists (born 1928–1945):** Emphasize respect, standards, and processes.

- **Baby Boomers (born 1946–1960):** Emphasize opportunities to solve problems, be challenged, and gain promotion.

- **Generation Xers (born 1961–1980):** Emphasize work-life balance, interesting and meaningful work, and development opportunities.

- **Generation Yers (born 1981–2000):** Emphasize fast decision making, stimulating work, teams, learning, and change.[2]

Look for Great Prospects in Usual and Unusual Places

The days of posting a job opening then sitting back and waiting for resumes are over. To meet your business objectives with this employee, launch an aggressive candidate prospecting campaign. Look in the usual places. Look in unusual places.

Cross Boundaries to Find Innovative Thinkers

If you are looking for innovative thinking, cross-pollinate and cross boundaries. Think about different industries, generations, nationalities, and cultures. Find niches in minority and community organizations and publications. Look for candidates in new talent pools like blogs, Facebook, Twitter, Bebo, Friendster, Orkut. University career sites can give you access to strong people with backgrounds you may never have considered. Make a list of every channel you can think of. Ask people on your team for more ideas. Work with your HR partner to flag sources your organization has used before, and those you haven't. Incorporate a few new channels as tests.

Market Directly to Known Top Performers

The top performers you really want are likely to be employed and pretty content in their current situations in either your organization or another. It is quite likely they are being or have been actively pursued by competitors, so they may be annoyed as opposed to flattered by a recruiting approach. Think relationship, not transaction, when you think about employed top performers. Think of ways to nurture an ongoing relationship so that when and if they are ready to make a move, you are at the top of their list and easy to approach. Keep the channels of communication open so you can alert them to opportunities in your organization in a nonintrusive manner. Employed, *nonactive job seekers* don't read want ads. You have to find them. Prospect by identifying them before you have an opening, and cultivate a relationship over time. A long-term relationship building process with employed top performers can significantly improve your candidate slate.

Start by creating a database of top people who are in roles you employ currently. This does not have to be complicated. A spreadsheet or simple database program is an adequate platform. Find top prospects by:

- Getting ideas from your organization's internal talent management and succession planning processes
- Offering referral bonuses to people in your organization who supply you with the names of top performers (particularly in specialist fields; top performers know other top performers)
- Participating in industry network groups (online and off)
- Prospecting at conferences, industry events, trade shows
- Being active on social networking sites
- Asking vendors and other external stakeholders for names of top performers
- Getting involved in industry associations
- Adding your own ideas

Build your relationship with known top performers inside and outside your organization with steady, ongoing communication. Leverage *excuses to contact* in order to gain enough direct experience to qualify or disqualify prospects for future opportunities with your organization. When you have an opening, give your qualified relationship prospects a courtesy call at the start of your search. Even if individuals aren't ready to consider a move to your organization, they will appreciate the special consideration. Keep building relationships until you have another employment opportunity to offer. Support your relationship management efforts by building your employment brand (see the employment brand section later in this chapter) so top performers can independently validate all the good things you say about your organization. Top performer relationship management contacts might include:

- Opportunities to network with business leaders in your company
- Invitations to participate in events sponsored by your organization
- Value-added publications written by your organization (white papers, etc.)

TIME-SAVER

Breadth of prospecting leads to more candidates, more choices, and fewer restarts of sourcing efforts.

To Build Your Slate, Cast a Wide Net—Use a Pre-qualification System to Pick Out the Gems

Some top prospects are, of course, in transition. Some you just won't be able to identify with your target marketing effort. So cast a wider net to find additional prospects. Before you post opportunities on Web sites and let the recruiters loose, work with your HR partner (if you have one) to create a job-specific prospect-scoring system based on your recruiting brief. You, your HR partner, or someone else will need to score and prioritize the resumes that come in. Think through the nominal number or the percentage of highest scoring resumes you will review in depth. If you take a less structured approach to prequalification, you risk taking too much time to make the first cut. If you delay interviewing and reaching offer decisions, you could let top candidates slip away to competitive offers.

A good recruiting brief (as described in chapter 3) spells out required talents, skills, and knowledge. Some of the skills can be assessed without an interview—particularly the technical and business skills. Some knowledge hurdles can be assessed without an interview: education, training, experience, and qualifications. Interviewing well takes time. It is far better to invest that time in candidates who meet the minimum qualifications than to waste it on people who don't.

Our point? Pre-screen people who don't meet your minimum qualifications, and make them go away even before you interview them. Check that they've actually earned the degrees they claim on their resume. It's easy to check, and you will, unfortunately, be surprised how many people exaggerate education.

SIMPLE PROSPECT SCORING

Do a rough rating of candidates' knowledge and experience by comparing what's on their resumes with the knowledge and experience sections of your recruiting brief. While this scale and what you will use during full evaluations are the same, we suggest you hold out for people with strong or outstanding knowledge and experience at this point to give you a larger margin for error.

5 = Outstanding strengths

4 = Strong evidence

3 = Enough evidence to support a hire

2 = Evidence that does not support a hire

1 = No evidence; this doesn't mean there is no evidence—just that none was found

TIME-SAVER

A clear scoring system allows you to weed out people who don't have the strengths you need before interviewing them. More candidates + fewer interviews means you are focusing your time on interviewing the highest potential candidates.

With worldwide communication flourishing on the Web, finding candidates is as easy as it is impossible to get exclusive access to top candidates. Ways to prospect for employees on the Web are included at the end of this chapter. Here are some thought starters:

- Create a candidate friendly Web site. List current job opportunities and categories of potential future job openings. Offer something in return for names and contact information.
- Post job openings on large job boards and specialist job boards.
- Tap into thought leadership groups by posting business problems that are pertinent to your job opening on news groups. Look for people who respond with great ideas or approaches. These people may be good candidates or they may be able to refer you to others who are.
- Use new technologies like *spiders* and *snakes* to search for prospect names, e-mail addresses, and resumes. Specialty search services, such as Trovix (www.trovix.com) and NimbleCat (www.nimblecat. com/ncmain.php4) can score online resumes against your job requirements.
- Hold dialogues with potential prospects using social networking, blogging, and Internet forums. Younger job seekers, in particular, expect to learn what they want to learn and ask prospective employers what they want to ask. To build a powerful slate of younger candidates, provide a meaningful and personal candidate experience from the first contact.
- Place motivating ads (print and digital).
- Use internal referral programs, and cultivate organization-wide responsibility for ongoing recruiting efforts.

- Post Internet videos (Google uses these).
- Create Second Life avatars (IBM uses these).
- Network.
- Use professional recruiters.

About Recruiters

- **Staffing agencies** hire people to work for the agency and then sub-contract them out to work for their clients. Organizations pay the agency, which then pays the employees. These relationships can be part-time, full-time, temporary, semipermanent, or temp to full with a buy-out provision to transfer the employee onto the organization's payroll. (Generally, staffing agencies work on entry- or lower-level jobs.)

- **Contingency recruiters** conduct searches for new employees and then get paid contingent on successful completion of the search. (Generally, contingency recruiters work on midlevel management jobs.)

- **Retained recruiters** are retained by organizations to find a new employee for an organization. Generally some or their entire fee is paid whether they actually complete the search or not. (Generally, retained recruiters work on more senior-level executive jobs.)

- **Outplacement/career agents** are paid by the candidate, prospective employee, or their previous employer. They work for the candidate to help them find their next role. (There is a whole range of outplacement services for people in a whole range of positions and levels.)

If you are going to use a recruiter, pick the right type and the right individual or firm and be prepared to manage your recruiting partner. David Lord is one of the world's experts on recruiters.

Contingency and retained search firms and in-house recruiters use research to help build their candidate pool. Sheila Greco is one of the luminaries in the candidate research field and has some useful perspective on how you should think about research whether you are

GUEST EXPERT

David Lord on Recruiters[3]

David Lord founded Executive Search Information Services in 1995, in response to requests from corporations for better information about executive recruiters and best practices in working with them. Since then, he has helped more than 100 Fortune 500 corporations improve their effectiveness in recruiting at senior levels.

We caught up with David in October 2008 at the "Executive Talent: A Global Perspective" search-consult conference in Frankfurt, Germany. He had eight prescriptions for people who are using outside search firms to help with their recruiting:

1. Focus on the real business case for managing search activity: higher completion rates, faster searches, higher quality candidates, and added value from search partnerships.

2. Avoid being driven by reducing search fees. If you really want the best talent, you probably want the best search consultants finding it and evaluating it for you, and the best search consultants don't need to discount their fees.

3. Get top management buyin. You can't manage executive recruiting without it.

4. Gather information rigorously on outcomes of all search engagements and use it to inform the search firm selection process.

5. Do not rush into a request-for-proposal/preferred-provider program. First, spend some time managing and standardizing the process of selecting and engaging search firms.

6. Generate the engagement letter and use fixed fees. It's your chance to spell out the process the way you want it carried out, addressing all issues important to you, setting the schedule of what will happen when, and educating all parties on their roles. Fair (not discounted) fixed fees are cleaner and crisper than percentage fees and should include all expenses except preapproved travel.

7. Gradually consolidate search activity into partnerships with a short list of large and small firms.

8. Separate the oversight of retained search from contingency recruiting. Retained search (exclusive to you) is a management consulting service. Contingency recruiting is one of many forms of candidate identification; no more, no less.[4]

doing it yourself, working with in-house recruiters, or working through outside recruiters.

GUEST EXPERT

Sheila Greco on Research[5]

How do you see the staffing industry adjusting to keep costs down and broaden its value?

1. We are seeing companies that are being strategic, proactive, and methodical as it relates to hiring. The days of handing over 3 to 5 candidates for a specific rec and saying, "here you go" are over. Many hiring managers want to be a part of the process and want to be shown the research, the pipeline from the targeted companies, how the potential qualified candidates compare and contrast with to each other, their respective teams, and the available talent universe. Methodical, yes, but very smart. Companies are looking for ways to keep costs down while still recruiting top talent. By using this methodical approach, the research can be used again and again thus creating value long-term.

2. Building and keeping relationships: Company executives really want those long-term partners who can help them. Hiring managers and recruiting professionals alike want a team approach and value the results that it produces.

3. Today, more so than in the past, successful recruiters are looked at as experts and partners. The respect has been earned, and we are now invited to have a seat at the conference table! Hiring managers have learned to respect what it takes to find the candidates, and we have conditioned them to listen to what we have to say. A great example is the fact that we have them understanding the value of tools that are now available: ATS, research and recruiting tools, and online communities. The executives are more on board with us! Great job, guys and gals.

4. Last, we are seeing many top companies across several industries going through the exercise of making sure their internal teams are staffed with the best in the industry. It is not surprising to have leaders take a peek at their competitors, their staff, and compare it to their own. If necessary, we are seeing them pluck the good ones from others.[6]

Speed Is an Advantage—Create Your Slate Against a Tight Time Line

Timing can be everything. Approaching a top performer at just the right moment can cinch the recruitment opportunity. Moving quickly through prospecting to recruitment to interviewing to offer can protect you from losing top-performer prospects. Assembling your full slate over a short period of time can give you leverage when you negotiate with your lead candidates because you have many good choices in hand.

HOT TIP

Utilize parallel processing; don't recruit sequentially. Broadly source a number of qualified candidates all at the same time to end up with a viable slate.

It's hard to overemphasize how many times we've seen people fall into the sequential recruiting trap. On the surface, it appears easier, faster, and more cost efficient. Wrong. Following each lead candidate through to an end point denies you the opportunity to think win-win or no deal with your lead candidate that comes from having viable backups.

TIME-SAVER

Hold your allies accountable for hitting the agreed time line. Calendar management is a critical component of parallel processing.

Tool 4.2 Candidate Sourcing provides a framework for thinking through different ways to source candidates. Tool 4.3 Candidate Tracking provides an easy framework for tracking candidates through the process.

Tool 4.2
Candidate Sourcing (Downloadable)

Recruiters

Type	Names	Relationship
Internal	Human Resources	Peer
External	H₂O Recruiting	Retained—$25,000
External	Whatever You Need Recruiting	Contingency—30%

Direct Marketing

Category	List	Action
Personal contacts	My address book	E-mail, call Meg and Norb
	Vendor	Call
	Human Resources contacts	
Groups	H₂O industry group	Attend meetings, e-mail request
	Farmers' guilds	E-mail request
	Community chest	Attend next meeting
	College of Water Supply alumni	E-mail request
Events	May: product supply conference	Attend and collect business cards

---

Social Networking

Site	Action
LinkedIn	Post "working on," Water Group bulletin board
Facebook	Update page

Advertising

Channel	Placement	Ad Creative
Company Web sites	Company Web site	Help wanted in Jobs tab
	Company candidate Web site	Job profile page
Industry web sites	www.WaterIndustry.com	Digital space ad creative #1
School web sites	www.LocalCollege.com	Digital space ad creative #1
	Monster.com	Listing #1
Job boards on the web	www.WaterJobBoard.com	Listing #2

Print publications	College of Water alumni magazine	Space ad creative #1
	Town paper	Space ad creative #1
	H_2O industry news	Space ad creative #2
Events	May: product supply conference	Attend and collect business cards

	Other	

Channel	**To Source**	**Next Step**
Web	Search position keywords	Contact top names, lead sources
Web	Questions on discussion boards	Contact people with intriguing responses
Web	Spiders and snakes resume search	Direct contact

Tool 4.3

Candidate Tracking (Downloadable)

Candidate	Initial Interview	Follow-up Communication	Second Interview	Follow-up Information	Offer	Status
Abigail	June 3	June 4	June 10	TBD		
Bryan	June 3	June 4	June 10	TBD		
Chas	June 3	June 4	June 10	TBD		
Delilah	June 3	June 4	June 10	TBD		
Edgar	June 3	June 4	June 10	TBD		
Francine	June 3	June 4	June 10	TBD		

Take creating your slate to the next level by creating a culture of continuous sourcing. Direct and train your managers to always be on the lookout for potentially good additions to their teams, internally and externally. Managers will improve their sourcing knowledge and skills and build a very strong pool of potential candidates for future opportunities.

Summary and Indicated Actions

1. Market before you buy. This chapter is about creating the slate, not narrowing it (which we'll do next). Everything communicates 24/7 forever. So drive your employment brand throughout this process.

2. Start with the recruiting brief as a tool to help guide your efforts and help you communicate the opportunity in a way that allows prospects to self-qualify—particularly when it comes to cultural fit.

3. Put together and implement a comprehensive prospect candidate campaign looking for candidates in usual and unusual places across industry, generational, national, cultural, and mindset boundaries.

4. Market directly to known top performers by building long-term relationships.

5. Use a simple pre-qualifying system.

6. Hit your time line milestones so you can manage the most promising candidates in parallel instead of sequentially.

Focus

- *Manager:* Inform and support HR's recruiting efforts. Source, source, source.
- *Human Resources:* Deliver candidates who fit the recruitment brief within the time line.

Evaluate Candidates Against the Recruiting Brief While Pre-Selling and Pre-Boarding

Recruit

Total Onboarding Program (TOP)				
Align>	Acquire>	Accommodate>	Assimilate>	Accelerate>
			Day One	IV. Enable and Inspire
		III. Big Head Start		
	II. Recruit Make the right offer, and close the right sale the right way. (6) Evaluate candidates against the brief while pre-selling and pre-boarding. (5) Create a powerful state of potential candidates. (4)			
I. Prepare				

Interview in a way that communicates and demonstrates your employment brand.

The tricky part of this stage of the Total Onboarding Program is that you have to think about buying and selling at the same time. The people you are interviewing don't have to do that. They can sell first, get you to offer them the job, and then decide whether to buy. In that light, we're going to split this chapter in two sections. We'll talk about pre-selling in section I, then interviewing and assessing in section II.

Section I—Pre-Sell While You Buy

Treat Them the Way You Are Going to Treat Them

We're not suggesting you pretend to be anything other than what you are. We are suggesting you treat the people you are recruiting and interviewing with the same respect that you will treat them with once they are employees, consistent with your employment brand. If you tend to be abrupt with your employees, go ahead and treat people you are recruiting the same way. At least they will know what they're getting into. If you aren't abrupt with employees, don't be abrupt with the people you are recruiting. Don't go too far the other way either. You don't want people to accept jobs under false pretenses and then quit when they discover that reality doesn't match their expectations.

Some of you have probably heard the story about the guy who died and then got to spend one day in heaven and one day in hell before choosing his final destination. After being treated to an amazingly wonderful day in hell, he decides to stay, only to be subjected to endless torture from then on. When he asks about this, he's informed that the good stuff is reserved for the people in the process of being recruited and ends once they sign up.

To be fair, most people on earth do not set out to mistreat recruits. Recruiting missteps tend to be crimes of neglect and miscommunication rather than crimes of intent. This is why thinking things through, communicating, and coordinating recruiting efforts is so important.

HURDLE

Buying and Selling at the Same Time

- **Problem:** Hiring organizations can lose new employees even before they extend the job offer.

- **Solution:** Treat recruiting like the strategically important exercise it is. Treat interviewees with the same respect you treat offerees or new employees.

Let's break this down into things to do before, during, and after the interviews. Every step of the recruiting process should be used as an opportunity to communicate, demonstrate, and live your employment brand.

Before the Interviews

It's entirely possible that your new employee's first contact with your organization will be with someone who doesn't work for your organization. This could be an on-campus career advisor, search firm, customer, or supplier. Or his or her first contact could be through the web or a recruiting brochure. Hopefully, whatever and whomever is talking about your organization to the recruit conveys useful information about your organization in a fair and reasonable way.

Help recruits prepare for their interviews. Generally, you care less about how well they interview than about how well they will perform on the job (unless interviewing is one of the required performance strengths). Helping candidates prepare for interviews is in everyone's best interests:

Too Much

- Making promises that can't be fulfilled. Luring people in with jobs that don't exist.

Just Right

- Painting a fair picture of the organization and role.
- Giving recruits information about the person or people with whom they will meet.
- Setting recruits up to have the best possible interview.
- Arranging travel and lodging, if required. Or at least giving recruits workable directions.

Too Little

- Neglecting to answer recruits' questions.
- Leaving recruits to their own devices to get to town/facility.

During the Interviews

The greeter or first interviewer should set the expectations for the interviews, letting recruits know how things are going to be handled and how the interviews will run:

Too Much

- Making false promises. Never promise something you can't deliver, including follow-up schedules, job offers, and so on.
- Offering an unsustainable welcome. One manager had recruits show up at his office at 1:00. His office was in Windsor, England, across the street from Windsor Castle where there was a parade every day at 1:00 to mark the changing of the guard. He'd tell recruits and other important guests that he'd arranged the parade for them. Not everyone believed him.

Just Right

- Making sure that the person who will greet recruits knows they are coming and knows where they should go. Someone should set expectations for the visit, describe schedule changes, and be prepared to meet the recruits' needs.
- Making sure everyone who interviews recruits is prepared, on time, and engaged. Recruits know when people are reading their resumes for the first time during the interview. They feel slighted when people are late. They can never be sure if a disengaged interviewer is looking down on them, the process, or the organization. Whichever it is, it sends the wrong signal.
- Using targeted selection and behavioral interviews. You can tell the recruit what you are looking for and help them communicate their best examples of those behaviors.(We'll talk about these in the second half of the chapter, but the point for now is that these tend to be relatively low stress.)
- Conducting two-way conversations as much as possible. You are not selling. But you *are* pre-selling.

- Offering downtime for recruits to catch their breath and collect their thoughts is valuable. Giving them a place to do that—an office with a phone and an Internet connection is even better.
- Giving recruits time to replenish and relieve themselves periodically. Making sure someone is feeding them lunch and giving them drinks. Making sure they have time to use the facilities (and know where to find them).
- Remembering that someone needs to say goodbye. Could be the last interviewer. Could be the recruit's shepherd for the day. Doesn't matter who it is. Just so that there's some closure and clarification offered about the next steps.

Too Little

- Sending them to the wrong place or not informing reception that they are coming. Not being prepared for them to show up early.
- Conducting one-way, pressure interviews.

HOT TIP

Use the interviews to pre-sell candidates *and* stakeholders.

Having future stakeholders interview prospective new employees gives them some ownership in the hiring decision and, therefore, in the employee's future success. This works well for stakeholders up and across.

Do not do this with people who are going to work for the new employee because it sets up uncomfortable initial interactions between employee and future boss.

Follow Up

This one's simple. Do what you say you are going to do, when you say you are going to do it. There's no excuse for leaving recruits out in the cold. You either want them to consider your offer, come back for another round of interviews, or say nice things about you to others.

Tool 5.1
On-Site Interview Day Plan (Downloadable)

Ahead of Time

Interview day selected	*June 3*
Interviewers scheduled	*Anna, Bart, Jill, Charlie, Devon*
Travel and other logistics set	*No travel required. Will get self to ops center.*
Pre-reading delivered to candidate (Logistics and schedule, interviewers' bios, organizational propaganda)	*Deliver May 30*
Pre-reading delivered to interviewers (Schedule, recruiting brief, candidate bios, interview guide/evaluation form)	*Deliver May 30*
Welcome note/package at hotel/home	*Package to Delilah's home*
Welcome sign in lobby/reception area	*No sign since interviewing several people on same day and want to preserve confidentiality across interviewees*

The Visit

Pre-interview dinner (when, where, who with?)	*Skip—no travel*
Pre-start breakfast (when, where, who with?)	*With Gina who is managing day*
Welcome (who?)	*Gina over breakfast*
Morning interviews	*9:00 Anna, 10:00 Charlie, 11:30 Devon*
Morning break (when?)	*11:00 in visitors' office in ops center*
Lunch (when, where, who with?)	*12:30 with Gina*
Afternoon interviews	*1:30 Jill, 3:00 Bart (optional)*
Afternoon break (when?)	*2:30 in visitor's office in ops center*
Close/wrap up/good-bye (who?)	*Gina at either 2:30 or 4:00*

Post-Visit

Follow-up note (package?)	*Note from Gina about process (and invite to final interviews as appropriate)*

SIGNS AND SYMBOLS WE LIKE

Treat people you are interviewing the way you want to be treated. Go out of your way to make sure interviewees are prepared, welcomed, listened to, fed, watered, and sent on their way knowing what to expect.

- **Message:** We value you as an individual. We appreciate your interest in our organization.

- **Action:** Prepare interviewers and candidates for the most productive interviews possible.

Prototypical Interview Day

We designed Tool 5.1 to work for one candidate or a group of candidates that are interviewing for the same position. Plan the interview day to make the best evaluation of the candidates and give candidates the best impressions of your organization.

Section II—The Evaluation Process

Evaluation consists of five steps, all flowing out of the recruiting brief. Utilize the recruiting brief to:

1. Screen candidates.
2. Interview candidates.
3. Compare data across interviewers and candidates.
4. Probe deeper to validate evidence of strengths.
5. Select those candidates to whom you will make an offer.

STOP

If you have not completed a recruiting brief and gotten stakeholders aligned behind it, do *not* proceed. Go back, and complete the work in chapter 3. You cannot evaluate candidates effectively unless people are in agreement about what you are looking for.

NOTE TO HR

You should probably act as process owner for interviewing and evaluating. Make sure things happen in an orderly, disciplined fashion and that people show up in the right places at the right times. You should also drive consensus on the organization's overall definition of strengths and which strengths are important for which jobs. This is particularly important because you need to hire people not just for their first job, but also for a career with your organization that will span many jobs.

Screening Interviews

Bill Noll has developed an excellent way to screen candidates. His behavioral profiling process utilizes a structured interview format of open-ended questions and can accurately predict an individual's future performance in a specific position by identifying 29 work behavioral traits/tendencies in the areas of management, sales, and support services. The questionnaires used in the interview process include predetermined sets of terms/phrases which interviewers are trained to listen for during responses. These terms/phrases have been developed on the basis of numerous concurrent, as well as predictive, criterion-related studies.

GUEST EXPERT

Bill Noll on Behavioral Interviews[1]

Having the right information can prevent you from making the wrong decisions.

A bad hire is costly both in terms of time and money. Behavioral profiling can give hiring managers more information up front about a potential employee, enabling you to make more intelligent hiring decisions. Additionally, this information enables individuals to express their talents in positions that maximize their satisfaction, productivity, and contribution.

Themes

- **Value system themes:** Mission, Belief, Responsibility, Ethics
- **Relationship themes:** Woo, Team, Relater, Empathy
- **Energy level themes:** Work Orientation, Stamina, Kinesthetic
- **Support staff themes:** Pride, Detail, Mastery
- **Sales:** Focus, Courage, Communication, Gestalt, Ego, Persuasion
- **Management:** Growth Orientation, Developer, Individualized Perception, Delegator, Stimulator, Arranger, Performance Orientation, Sophistication, Innovation

THE PROCESS

Noll's behavioral profiling interview includes approximately 130 structured, stress-free questions with specific "listen fors" that are based on the responses to the answers furnished by proven top achievers in each theme or characteristic. It produces ideas about how to help the person maximize his or her overall strengths and manage around limitations and compare strength levels across interviewees.

The Selection Cone

Noll's research indicates that each person has a comfort level with individuals who are more or less talented than themselves. Some individuals are very picky and have a small selection cone while others can work with just about anyone. On the Talent Level Chart that follows, the illustration of the selection cone shows the first individual in the Recommended category hiring someone less talented than himself, and that person in turn then hired someone less talented than herself thus causing the decline of talent within the organization. With a structured interview process, it is possible to hire someone as capable or more capable than the hiring leader and therefore strengthen the organization by promoting positive growth rather than allowing natural deterioration over a period of time. The tendency among many people is to compromise on hiring, which becomes more magnified as each person continues to compromise. It is only slowed by an accidental *hire up* rather than a *hire down*.

Selection Cones

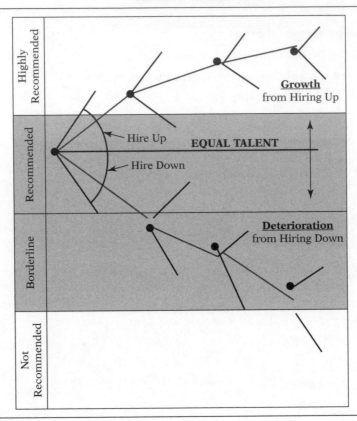

NOTE TO HR

You can be invaluable here. Hold a mirror up to hiring managers and prevent them from wasting everyone's time interviewing unqualified people, no matter how strong their neighbor's sister's dog walker's recommendation.

Interview Candidates

We use a targeted selection/behavioral approach to interviewing with great success. Our approach included formal post-interview debriefs, gathering information outside the interviews, and post-interview follow-ups with candidates to learn even more.

There are only three questions in any interview. Every question you've ever asked anyone in any interview anytime, anywhere, for any job is a subset of one of these three questions:

1. Can you do the job?
2. Will you love the job?
3. Can I stand working with you?

In other words: strengths, motivation, and fit. That's it. Those three. There aren't any others.

It's even easier than that. You can't really ask people if they will love the job. You can't ask people if you can stand working with them. So, ask questions about their strengths, and derive answers to your other questions.

Now, to make things even easier, you don't care about their strengths in general. All you care about is whether they have the specific strengths you identified in the recruiting brief as being most important for the job you are filling.

The magic of behavioral interviewing is that it is based on the premise that past behavior is the best predictor of future behavior. Thus, interviewing gets boiled down to asking candidates to give you examples of past behavior that demonstrate the strengths you are looking for. This approach is effective and positive because it changes a potentially adversarial, challenging interaction to a joint problem-solving exercise. You actually want to do everything you can to help the people you are interviewing find the best possible examples and evidence of their strengths.

If they've got the strengths, they can provide the evidence.

If they don't have the strengths, they won't be able to provide the evidence no matter how good you or they are at the different sides of interviewing.

One leader's interviews got simpler and simpler over the years. They generally followed a pattern like this:

I'm going to do a behavioral interview. I'm looking for evidence of strengths in what you've done in the past. I'll tell you the strength I'm looking for. You give me an example. It's helpful if you use a STAR framework in your answer:

ST: Situation (Briefly—just enough to help me understand your actions.)

A: Action (Elaborate here. What you did. Use the word "I.")

R: Result (Briefly—just enough to show me the value of what you did.)

The questions aren't important. The answers are. So if I ask a question that doesn't trigger a good example, let's skip that one and find another way to get at examples of your strengths.

Another leader's marketing interviews are even simpler. They consist of one question that uncovers a wide array of strengths, "Give me an example of a time when you turned a consumer insight into a business success."

Answers to this question highlight many strengths:

- *Ability to identify consumer insights:* Analytical, Empathy, Ideation, Input, and Learner strengths
- *Ability to put together a strategic plan:* Deliberative, Focus, and Strategic strengths
- *Ability to rally a team around that plan:* Activator, Arranger, Command, Communication, Futuristic, Harmony, Includer, Positivity, and Self-Assurance strengths
- *Ability to manage the plan's execution:* Adaptability, Competition, Discipline, Relater, Responsibility, and Restorative strengths

(In this example, we use Gallup strengths definitions. You can use any system that works for you.)

Other people break interviews into a series of questions, each designed to get at one strength. Breaking strategic planning down could yield questions like:

- Give me an example of a time when you had to make an important decision. Tell me about the obstacles you anticipated and how you went about making the decision. I'm looking for *Deliberative* strengths.

- Give me an example of a time when you had to take a direction, follow through, and make necessary corrections to stay on track. I'm looking for your strengths in the area of *Focus*.

- Give me an example of a time when you had to evaluate alternative ways to proceed, identified the patterns and issues, and chose a way forward. I'm looking for *Strategic* strengths here.

By now, you get the point. Pick the strengths you are looking for. Ask for examples. Your part is just that easy. Tool 5.2 will help you plan and record your interviews.

Tool 5.2

Interview Guide (Downloadable)

Candidate	*Delilah*
Position (Grade)	*Associate Director of Aquatic Delivery (H_2O)*
Key communication points about organization	*We are an ecofriendly company that does important work. Our culture values expression of individuality, continual learning, and fun*
1. Team purpose	*Secure water supply*
2. Role priorities	*Strengthen transport system, reduce accidents, and manage transport process*
3. Organizational values	*Integrity, consistency (highly collegial)*

Strength ratings for this section are (1 = no evidence, 2 = evidence does not support hire, 3 = hirable, 4 = strong, 5 = outstanding)

Strength #1: *Achiever*

Question
Give me an example of a time where your stamina and hard work contributed to accomplishing a task.

Data
Strength: Apple transport system broken, damaging apples. Achievement: Got team to help me and worked through the night carrying apples down from the orchards to save the harvest. Result: 98% of apples harvested successfully (versus 90% normally)

Rating 4

Strength #2: *Discipline*

Question
Give me an example of a time when you had to deploy a disciplined routine and structure to a task

(continued)

Tool 5.2 (continued)
Interview Guide (Downloadable)

Data

Strength: Fallen apples needed to be picked up daily or they'd rot. Achievement: Deployed system where I picked up fallen apples on one side of orchard right before morning break and other side right before lunch. Result: Lost no apples to ground rot

Rating 3

Strength #3: *Focus*

Question

Give me an example of a time when you took direction, followed through, and made necessary corrections to keep a project on track.

Data

Strength: Was asked to improve apple hand-off process from pickers to transporters. Achievement: Talked to all the pickers to understand their issues and put in place process to pick baskets up every half hour. Didn't work. Changed system to have taller transporters empty baskets from top of ladders every 15 minutes. Result: Better flow

Rating 4

Gallup Strengths[2]

People strong in _____ have or do . . .

Achiever: Has stamina and works hard. Derives satisfaction from being busy and productive.

Activator: Can make things happen by turning thoughts into action. Often impatient.

Adaptability: Prefers to go with the flow. Now people. Takes things as they come and discovers the future one day at a time.

Analytical: Searches for reasons and causes. Thinks about all the factors that might affect a situation.

Arranger: Can organize, but also has a flexibility that complements this ability. Likes to figure out how all the pieces and resources can be arranged for maximum productivity.

Belief: Has certain core values that are unchanging → defined purpose for their life.

Command: Has presence. Takes control of situations and make decisions.

Communication: Finds it easy to put thoughts into words. Good conversationalists and presenters.

Competition: Measures their progress against the performance of others. Strives to win first place and revels in contests.

Connectedness: Has faith in the links between all things. Believes there are few coincidences and almost every event has a reason.

Consistency/Fairness: Has a keen awareness of the need to treat people the same by setting up clear rules and adhering to them.

Context: Enjoys thinking about the past. Understands the present by researching its history.

Deliberative: Takes serious care in making decisions or choices. Anticipates the obstacles.

Developer: Recognizes and cultivates potential in others. Spots signs of each small improvement and derives satisfaction from these improvements.

Discipline: Prefers routine and structure and the order they create.

Empathy: Can sense feelings of other people by imagining themselves in others' lives or situations.

Focus: Can take a direction, follow through, and make corrections that are necessary to stay on track. Prioritizes, and then acts.

Futuristic: Is inspired by the future and what it could be. Inspires others with their visions of future.

Harmony: Looks for consensus and agreement. Doesn't enjoy conflict.

Ideation: Fascinated by ideas. Able to find connections between seemingly disparate phenomena.

Includer/Inclusiveness: Accepting of others. Shows awareness of those who feel left out and makes an effort to include them.

Individualization: Intrigued with unique qualities of each person. Has a gift for figuring out how people who are different can work together productively.

Input: Has a craving to know more. Collects and archives all kinds of information.

Intellection: Enjoys intellectual activity. Introspective and appreciates intellectual discussions.

(continued)

(continued)

Learner: Has a desire to learn and continuously improve. Excited by the process of learning, rather than the outcome.

Maximizer: Focuses on strengths as a way to stimulate personal and group excellence. Seeks to transform something strong into something superb.

Positivity: Has an enthusiasm that is contagious. Upbeat and can get others excited about what they are going to do.

Relator: Enjoys close relationships with others. Achieves a deep satisfaction in working hard with friends to achieve a goal.

Responsibility: Has a psychological ownership of what they say they will do. Committed to stable values such as honesty and loyalty.

Restorative: Adept at dealing with problems. Good at figuring out what is wrong and resolving it.

Self-Assurance: Has an inner compass $\rightarrow$ confidence their decisions are right.

Significance: Wants to be important to others.

Strategic: Sees alternative ways to proceed. Patterns and issues.

Woo: Wins others over. Good at breaking the ice and connecting.

GUEST EXPERT

Oren Trask on Idea Ownership[3]

Oren Trask was CEO of media conglomerate Trask Industries. He was particularly gifted in choosing great people.

Behavioral interviews are useful . . . to a point. It's essential to separate out people who know how to interview from people who know how to deliver. There are a lot of people who can figure out how things happened in retrospect. There's a smaller subset of people that can make things happen in the moment.

I've found it's essential to go beyond the initial behavioral examples someone gives me in an interview to probe idea ownership. In a variation of the five levels of why, I look at levels of "How did you come up with the idea?"

Generating a Good Idea

Here's an example of exactly that: One man claimed to have grown his brand in Austria 30+ percent. George probed, "How did you accomplish that result?"

"We launched a new advertising campaign."

"Tell me about the advertising."

[He did.]

"Tell me about the underlying insight."

[He did.]

"How did you come up with the idea?"

"Actually, I didn't. The agency did."

"Okay, tell me how you worked with the agency."

"I didn't. It was the global agency."

"Okay. What was your role in the advertising?"

"We customized it for Austria."

"Tell me about that customization."

[He did.]

"Tell me about the underlying insight."

[He did.]

"How did you come up with the idea?"

"Actually, I didn't. The regional agency did."

"Okay, tell me how you worked with the regional agency."

"I didn't. They were managed out of Brussels."

"Okay, tell me what you did."

"We did the local media."

"Tell me about the local media."

[He did]

"Tell me about why it worked."

[He did]

"How did you come up with the idea?"

"Actually, I didn't. The media agency did."

"Okay, tell me how you worked with the media agency."

"I didn't. They were managed out of Zurich."

As far as George could tell, this guy hadn't done anything beyond being in the right place at the right time. The question "How did you come up with the idea?" gave George what he needed to get below the surface of the results and his understanding of the results to get at what the candidate had actually done or not done.

We urge you to use this question practically word for word. Don't settle for generalities. Probe until you can find the specific, particular moment when the connection was made, the impulse, the *ah-ha*, eureka moment when the idea was born. Look for someone connecting two previously unconnected things. For example:

- Superglue that didn't work + small pieces of paper = Post-it notes.
- Research reports + spreadsheets in the same program = the Bloomberg system.
- Collectibles and collectors + the Internet = eBay.

HOT TIP

Ask, "How did you come up with the idea?"

This is the best way we've found to differentiate between people who understand why things were successful and people who make things successful. You want the latter.

Compare Data Across Interviewers and Candidates

There are two questions:

1. Is this person hirable?
2. How do we rank all the hirable candidates?

Question one asks whether or not the candidate meets the minimum requirements. Question two asks you to put those candidates who meet the minimum requirements in rank order. You don't really want to narrow down to one candidate too quickly. You want to create a slate of preferred candidates so that you keep your backups viable.

Tool 5.2: Interview Guide and Tool 5.3: Interview Debrief work together. Use these to rate candidates against the required strengths, motivation, and fit. Each interviewer collects data and assigns a rating on the strengths he or she probes and provides a judgment on motivation and fit:

5 = Evidence of outstanding strengths.

4 = Strong evidence.

3 = Enough evidence to support a hire.

2 = Evidence that does not support a hire.

1 = No evidence; note this doesn't mean there is no evidence—just that none was found.

After all the interviews are complete, the interviewers should get together to compare notes and ratings. Use Tool 5.3 to frame these conversations. More likely than not, different interviewers will have found different evidence of strengths and applied different ratings. Accept the highest rating supported by the evidence, not the average, and not the consensus rating. If even one person found "outstanding" evidence, that evidence exists. Remember, this is not an exercise in judging peoples' ability to interview (on either side of the table). It's an exercise in uncovering evidence of strengths. The output is a slate of candidates to look at more closely.

Tool 5.3

Interview Debrief (Downloadable)

Rating _____

(1 = no evidence, 2 = evidence does not support hire, 3 = hirable, 4 = strong, 5 = outstanding)

Candidate	Strength 1	Strength 2	Strength 3	Motivation	Fit	Comments/ Actions
	Achiever	Discipline	Focus			
Alger	3	4	3	3	3	Viable—probe deeper
Beth	5	2	2	4	3	Refer to others in org
Chuckie	3	2	3	2	2	Cut loose
Delilah	4	3	4	4	4	Leader—probe deeper
Edgar	3	3	3	3	3	Barely acceptable— probe

Probe Deeper to Validate Evidence

Now that you've got a slate, it's time to probe deeper. There are a number of ways to do this: reference checks, background checks, follow-up conversations, and what candidates do and say after the interviews can give you much of what you are looking for—if you probe with discipline and thoroughness.

Reference Checks

Most people know they should do reference checks. Few people do them well. It comes down to who you talk to and what you ask. In general, talking to the people that candidates suggest you talk to for references is not going to be sufficient. Candidates will probably steer you to the people who will give the best references. You will want to find a good cross section of past bosses, peers, and subordinates and ask them about the strengths you probed during the interviews. Ask for examples. Look for evidence of strengths.

GUEST EXPERT

Geoffrey Smart on Reference Checking[4]

Thoroughness is critical to topgrading (finding the few A players). One tactic that is particularly useful for keeping executive candidates honest in interviews—the "threat of reference check" (TORC) tactic. It works like this:

> At the beginning of the interview, tell the candidate "We may ask for your help in setting up reference calls with some of your past bosses and colleagues, if that is okay with you." By establishing the fact that you may talk with past bosses and colleagues and implying that you are going to verify the information they give you, you will get much more honest and less exaggerated information from the candidate.
>
> Then, when you are talking about a certain job they had, you might ask, "What was your boss' name?" "What was it like to work with her?" "What do you think she is likely to say were some of your biggest strengths in that job and why?" "What do you think she will say were some of your areas for improvement in that job and why?"
>
> Then go back and talk to three past bosses, two past subordinates, and two past peers to see if you get the same read on strengths, areas for improvement, and overall performance.[5]

While you may not want to follow Geoff's prescription to talk to everyone, it's pretty clear that thorough reference checking can reduce risks of failure later. Shame on you, if you don't uncover personal risks during reference checking. Shame on you, if you don't get a real read on the candidate's strengths, motivation, and fit: what they are really good at, what really makes them tick, what groups they work best with.

Background Checks

The depth of background checks will vary with the level of the position and the downside of failure. Things to consider are:

- Past employment verification
- Address checks
- Citizenship/visa/work permit checks
- Education verification (if you did not do this before the interviews)
- Legal background checks both on the criminal and civil side. Useful to know what crimes they've been charged with and convicted of. Useful to know whom they've sued, who's sued them, and any other actions
- Credit checks. Useful to know past credit history and current status
- More in-depth checks may be warranted in some cases including stock or corporate ownerships. Useful to know if your candidate has a side business or potentially conflicting board memberships

Much of this is relatively easy and inexpensive. There are organizations that will do all of this for you. At the same time, laws and regulations about which of these you can do when vary by geography. Check those laws and regulations before you do anything. At the very least, use search engines and social networking sites on the Web to gather more information about your candidates. Tool 5.4 is a good way to keep track of what you learn during reference and background checks.

The Legend of Bunk Bed Billy   Billy had been hired as a shipping assistant. One of the things the company liked about him was that he'd spent two years in Argentina as a missionary. He'd talked about that during his interviews.

A few weeks after Billy joined the company, the guy at the desk next to him, Joe, lost his wallet. Someone was using Joe's credit card in clothing stores and a hardware store where that person bought a bunk bed. "A bunk bed!" Joe yelled into the phone. "I don't even have kids. I'd never buy a bunk bed."

Then someone tried to use Joe's credit card to take money out of the cash machine in the company's lobby. The transaction was on the security tape. Joe recognized Billy.

Tool 5.4

Reference/Background Check (Downloadable)

Candidate:	Delilah
Position:	Senior Associate Director of Aquatic Delivery (Grade H_2O)
University degree verications:	N.A.
Strengths required:	1. Achiever 2. Discipline

Source	Supervisors	Overall Batings	Comments
Previous supervisor	Judy	3	Did a nice job
Supervisor prior to that	Stan	4	One of our best
Supervisor prior to that	Ziva	3	Pleasure to work with
	Key Peers/ Allies/Customers		
1	Matilda	3	Always helpful
2	Michael	4	Gives extra effort
3	Mula	3	A good partner. (Just don't let her cut hair.)
	Direct Reports		
1	Dana	5	Best ever!
2	Deva	4	Tough, but good
3	Dipa	5	Kept us on track

Deep background checks (as appropriate):	Level II security clearance by water authority
Legal history:	No history of lawsuits either way
Criminal history:	Minor: speeding tickets, one disorderly conduct at a rock concert in a water park

It turned out that Billy's two years as a missionary were really spent in the state penitentiary for forging checks.

The company should have found that out before they hired Billy.

But then we wouldn't have "The Legend of Bunk Bed Billy" as a story for this chapter to help you remember to do background checks.

REALITY CHECK

Even though you won't necessarily tell candidates about your background checks, do them in a way that won't embarrass anyone at any time. Rational people won't be upset if you accessed public records to learn about them. You know where the legal, moral, and ethical boundaries are. Don't even get close to that line.

TIME-SAVER

Standard operating procedure is to do reference and background checks on the final candidate.

Parallel process this instead. Do reference and background checks on the most viable final candidates to help you make your final selection decision and set you up to move quickly if your first choice turns you down.

Follow-Up Conversations

If you need more information from candidates, talk to them. There's no rule about getting all the information in one interview. If something wasn't clear, clarify it. If there's an evidence gap, fill it. Follow-up conversations work on two levels: they help you learn more, and they keep candidates *warm*.

Some people use a three-conversation rule. No matter how much they are impressed with a candidate, they won't offer anyone a job until they've met with them on three separate occasions.

What Candidates Do and Say After Interviews

Pay attention to what candidates do to follow up with you. Do they write thank-you notes? Do they send their correspondence by e-mail, regular mail, or overnight mail? Are notes typed? Handwritten? Do candidates send supplemental information about areas that weren't clear? Do they follow up with questions? This is not a checklist of what candidates should do, just a reminder to be aware that everything communicates, and you can learn a lot from what candidates do and say or don't do and don't say after interviews.

Select a Candidate

Now you are ready to make your selection. You've got all the evidence. You've got other people's perspectives. You've probed deeper to learn more. Take in everything you have learned. Then, trust your judgment to create your final, ranked slate.

At this point, you still want a slate, instead of one superstar. Having options makes things better all the way around with your lead candidate, as you'll see in the next chapter.

MASTER CLASS

Take interviewing to the next level by setting aside one day each month for interviews. All appropriate managers should keep these days open whenever possible. A fixed, monthly interview day makes it easier to schedule candidates for interviews and gives managers an opportunity for regular, deliberate interview practice. The regularly occurring interview day also signals the importance of your Total Onboarding Program to the organization and potential employees.

Summary and Indicated Actions

Evaluating candidates is hard work and important work. Remember to buy and sell at the same time so you make careful selections and increase the probability of the lead candidate accepting your offer. Be disciplined in your approach to recruiting and interviewing. Always communicate, demonstrate, and live your employment brand to attract people who will move happily and smoothly into your organization.

Use the recruiting brief (Tool 3.2) to guide the following five steps:

1. Prescreen candidates.
2. Interview candidates.
3. Compare data across interviewers and candidates.
4. Probe deeper to validate evidence of strengths.
5. Select those candidates to be hired.

Focus

- *Manager:* Decide who you want to hire, and pre-sell at every step along the way.
- *Human Resources:* Manage the interview process. Provide a broader organizational perspective.

CHAPTER 6

Make the Right Offer, and Close the Right Sale the Right Way

Recruit

Total Onboarding Program (TOP)					
Align>	Acquire>	Accommodate>	Day One	Assimilate>	Accelerate>
				IV. Enable and Inspire	
		III. Big Head Start			
	II. Recruit Make the right offer, and close the right sale the right way. (6) Evaluate candidates against the brief while pre-selling and pre-boarding. (5) Create a powerful state of potential candidates. (4)				
I. Prepare					

Treat the offer as just one part of a strategic sale. The way you handle offers and support your new employees' due diligence efforts will impact the way they feel about you and your organization—with implications far beyond the yes or no. You want offerees to say "yes," if the move is right for them, their supporters, and the organization. You want them to say "no," if it's not.

This part is supposed to be easy. You mapped out the role and got stakeholders aligned around it. You found the most appropriate candidates. You and your colleagues conducted the interviews and background checks while pre-selling. The lead candidate proved his or her strengths, motivation, and fit with the organization. Now, it's entirely reasonable to expect the lead candidate to accept the job the moment you make the offer.

It could happen.

Don't count on it.

Actually, you don't really want it to happen.

We Want You—But We're Not Going to Tell You

The interviews were tough. That didn't bother Brenda at all. She expected interviews at a top-flight company like Tip-Top Products to be tough. They told her they'd get back to her in two weeks.

After three weeks, she called to get a status update. "We're sending you a letter today."

After another week, she called again. "We're so sorry. The letter got mangled in the copy room and never went out. We'll reprint it."

"Can you just tell me what it says?"

"We're offering you a job."

It probably won't surprise you to learn that Brenda did not end up accepting this job. The organization dug itself into a big hole before it started selling and was not able to recover despite putting a full-court press on Brenda.

Roles reverse at the moment of a job offer. The candidate moves from selling to buying. You move from buying to selling. While your pre-selling efforts will have helped, it's well worth your time to map out and implement a complete strategic selling effort that communicates, demonstrates, and lives your employment brand to move your lead candidate toward the right decision on a timely basis.

Before we get to the steps of a strategic sale, remember:

- You are selling. Your goal is to get the right candidate to accept the right offer.

- You do not want candidates to accept offers that aren't right for them. It is far better for everyone involved to have a candidate turn down an offer than accept, join, and fail early on. (Particularly when you have a powerful slate of backup candidates.)

- If a candidate is going to turn you down, you want that to happen sooner rather than later. The strength of your slate of backup candidates degrades over time. If your first-choice candidate turns you down quickly, you can extend an offer to your second choice. Your second choice may never know that he or she was the backup. If your first-choice candidate negotiates for several weeks before turning you down, you may have to start all over again.

- Candidates are not alone. Closing a strategic sale almost always involves getting to influencers as well as to the primary decision maker. Find them. Influence them.
- Run through the tape. Just because they're sold doesn't mean they will stay sold. Stick with your selling/communication campaign all the way through the first day on the job—and beyond.

With that in mind, here are the seven steps of a strategic sale (and the outline of this chapter).

Steps of a Strategic Sale

1. Identify the players and influencers in the decision-making process:
   - *Economic buyer:* The decision maker who can say yes—generally the new employee.
   - *User buyer:* The new employee.
   - *Technical buyer:* A person who can say "no" but can't say "yes"— family members.
   - *Coach:* A person who can influence the decision.
2. Pinpoint why the organization and role are right for this candidate. How will this organization and job absolutely meet the decision maker's needs, hopes, and desires better than other opportunities?
3. Spell out why the candidate is right for the organization and role.
4. Understand the candidate's concerns.
5. Understand influencers' needs, hopes, desires, and concerns.
6. Think through ways to alleviate the candidate's and influencers' concerns.
7. Develop and implement your selling campaign:
   - Verbal offer
   - Written offer
   - Help with due diligence
   - Follow-up phone calls

- Other live meetings
- Close the sale/targeted acceptance date
- Make sure the sale stays closed

1. Identify the Players and Influencers in the Decision-Making Process

Consider four different types of players: economic buyers, user buyers, technical buyers, and coaches. In this case, the economic buyer and user buyer are generally one and the same: the candidate. Technical buyers are those influencers who can say "no," but can't say "yes." They include past, present, and future family members. In some rare cases, family members are economic buyers because they have so much influence. Coaches include other influencers like mentors, colleagues, business partners, extended family members, and friends.

Take a broader rather than narrower view of influencers. Start by identifying as many as you can. Then focus on the most important people.

Lee accepted the job without reservations. Then her father got sick. The new job posed a dilemma because it required relocation. There was no Korean community near her new job. She couldn't leave her father alone and couldn't move him away from his friends in the Korean community with no way for him to make new Korean friends elsewhere. Lee changed her mind and turned down the job.

No one could have anticipated Lee's father's illness changing her decision. You are not going to identify all the possible influencers. Still, do try to identify as many as possible.

In our example in Tool 6.1, Delilah is the economic and user buyer. Her spouse, Samson, is a major influencer (technical buyer), as is Xenia, her mentor (coach). Tool 6.1 can help organize and track your thinking during the offer closing process.

2. Pinpoint Why the Organization and Role Are Right for the Candidate

Strategic selling is about problem solving and opportunity realization. You can't position your offer as your candidate's best choice until you understand what your candidate is looking for and running away from. Start with the candidate's needs, hopes, and desires. This shouldn't be hard, because these are a big part of what you've been trying to understand since first meeting the candidate.

Tool 6.1
Offer Closing Process (Downloadable)

Candidate:	*Delilah*

Position:	*Senior Associate Director of Aquatic Delivery (Grade H_2O)*
Key Influencers:	*Spouse, Samson (Technical Buyer); Mentor, Xenia (Coach)*

Why organization and role are right for candidate (overlap with needs, hopes, and desires):

Fits with Delilah's core values of doing good for others and valuing the environment.

Fits with Delilah's affinity for working in pairs in a sociable group with a hands-off manager.

Moves Delilah forward toward a future as director of product supply.

Why candidate is right for organization and role:

Delilah has required strengths as Achiever, Discipline, Focus (as well as Responsibility and Self-Assurance).

Delilah is a practiced water resource expert and physics expert.

Candidate's concerns:

Delilah is concerned about safety issues in role.

Delilah isn't sure how Jill is going to react to her.

Delilah is concerned about moving her family.

Key Influencers' needs, hopes, desires, and concerns:

Delilah's spouse, Samson, shares Delilah's concerns about safety and is worried about moving because he would have to switch jobs in a tough economy.

Her mentor, Xenia, recommended Delilah for the job. Xenia was Jack Jr.'s teacher in eighth grade. While Xenia is confident that Delilah and Jack Jr. can establish a good working relationship, she's concerned about Delilah's ability to get along with Jill.

Ways to alleviate concerns:

Provide safety improvement information.

Encourage Jill and Delilah to jump-start relationship.

Help Samson find a new job.

Verbal offer made	*By Anna*	*Jun 17*
Written offer delivered	*By Hal*	*Jun 18*

Assistance with due diligence—items for follow-up action:

Organization: Introduce Delilah to operational safety team so she can dig into safety improvements.

Give Delilah copy of latest organizational strategic plan.

Role: Arrange conversation between Delilah and Jill so they can get a jump start on their relationship.

Personal: Share results of behavioral strengths assessments *(continued)*

Offer Closing Process (Downloadable)

Calls:

Phone call to identify concerns still outstanding	From Anna	To Delilah	Jun 17
Other phone calls as appropriate	From Jill	To Delilah	Jun 19
	From Hal	To Samson	Jun 20

Other live meetings to alleviate concerns and drive messages about organization, role, candidate:
TBD

Target acceptance date:
Jun 24

All candidates have other options. Some can stay in their current job. Some have other offers. Some can keep looking for another job. Some have all of the above. So it's not good enough to understand how your offer meets your candidate's needs, hopes, and desires. You have to understand how your offer is better than competing options.

You've already done this work. Look back at your messages (Tool 2.3), your recruiting brief (Tool 3.2), and your employment brand (Tool 4.1). They contain the reasons the organization and role are right for the candidate.

Use Tool 6.1 to note where your purpose and values and how your work overlap with your candidate's needs, hopes, and desires. (In our example, the organization and role fit with Delilah's core values, play to her affinity for working in pairs with a hands-off manager, and move her forward toward becoming a director of product supply.)

3. Spell Out Why the Candidate Is Right for the Organization and Role

You've already done this work. Look at the information you've collected in your interview guide (Tool 5.2), in your interview debrief (Tool 5.3), and in your reference/background check guide (Tool 5.4). Be ready to answer the candidate's question "What specifically, about me, led to you offering me the job?" The candidate should ask this as part of his or her due diligence.

4. Understand the Candidate's Concerns

Note candidate concerns you've heard along the way. Every candidate has concerns. Some people are more open about sharing concerns. You should be most worried about the unstated ones, because you can't address what you aren't aware of. Probe deeply. Listen carefully to the candidate and his or her influencers to find concerns.

5. Understand Influencers' Needs, Hopes, Desires, and Concerns

Next, map out the same things for people who may influence the candidate and will be affected by whether the candidate takes the job. This is more difficult because you don't know them as well as you know the candidate (if at all). The best way to learn about influencers may be to ask the candidate about them. In some cases, you may be able to have direct conversations with the influencers—but only as part of your normal dealings with the candidate. Taking the candidate and his or her spouse or partner out to dinner between the offer and acceptance is a good way to get to know both of them and their needs, hopes, desires, and concerns. There are questions you can ask after making someone a job offer that you can't or shouldn't ask before then.

Pay attention to past, present, and future family members, taking a particularly broad view of the definition of *family*.

Past family members may include parents, spouses, children, and the like. While one good way to get my mother's blood to boil is to remind her that she's no longer part of my "nuclear family," some people are deeply involved in caring for aging parents. Ex-spouses and particularly ex-spouses with custody of children may limit a candidate's relocation and travel flexibility. At some point, children grow up and leave the nest. Still, some people will want to stay close to where their children live.

Present family members are especially influenced by and influential about a new job decision. In many cases, their needs, hopes, desires, and concerns are close to those of the decision maker. In other cases, trade-offs need to be made about things like dual careers, schools, housing, or friends. Make sure you help your offerees think these through.

Future family members may be harder to take into consideration—especially if they don't exist yet! Don't discount the impact boyfriends or girlfriends can have. Don't discount the power of a future vision that includes family members.

HOT TIP

Look beyond the candidate to the people influencing him or her.

Making the case to others involved in the job acceptance decision can mean the difference between a yes and a no.

---

6. Think Through Ways to Alleviate Candidate's and Influencers' Concerns

This is a critical piece. If you can't figure out how to alleviate the candidate's and his or her influencers' concerns, the candidate should probably not accept. You may even need to rescind the offer. It's far better to recognize a mistake now than after the candidate accepts. Ideally you will alleviate all concerns.

7. Develop and Implement Your Selling Campaign

Plan the whole selling campaign from verbal offer to target acceptance date. Sometimes you can compress selling into a day or two. Sometimes it will take several weeks. Think about a one-week process as the average campaign for the average job in the average company. One week is generally enough time for most candidates to consider a job offer, and it's not long enough to put you in jeopardy of losing too many backup candidates. You may or may not follow the plan exactly; but you do want to start by laying out who's going to communicate what to the candidate (and influencers) in what order, at what times, in what manner.

Verbal Offer

When you offer someone a job you are inviting him or her to follow you. You are asking them to change their professional lives. A job offer is a very personal event. So, the offer you extend needs to be as personal as you can make it. If you can make the offer in a face-to-face meeting, that's great. If you can't, then at least make it by phone. It's far more important to communicate your enthusiasm for being able to offer the candidate the job than it is to communicate the details of the offer at this point. Make your candidate feel valued.

David drove eight hours for his interviews and then eight hours back to Missouri. The next day he got a call from Sam asking if he'd come back for more conversations. But David was reluctant to do all that driving again. Sam asked, "Would you meet me halfway?" David did and got the job. He took the job partly because of Sam's going the extra step to meet him halfway and then offer him the job personally. Years later, he succeeded that very same Sam as Wal-Mart's second CEO.

SIGNS AND SYMBOLS TO CONSIDER ABOUT THE OFFER

While all leadership is personal, inviting someone to make a life change to come work for you is especially personal.

Make job offers face-to-face if you can to strengthen your personal connection.

- *Message.* We want you to join us.
- *Action.* Extend a personal invitation.

Written Offer
After you make the verbal offer, follow up immediately with a written offer that spells out the details. This doesn't have to be a 200-page contract; it could be a simple three-line e-mail. What's important is that the written offer is something that feels official.

NOTE TO HR

You should probably own the written offer. It's fine to have the hiring manager sign it. However, there probably needs to be a consistent way you word offers, compensation packages, and so on.

Assistance with Due Diligence

This one's a little counterintuitive. We suggest that you actively help your offer recipient with due diligence. There are two reasons for this. The most important reason is that you really do want your offer recipient to do due diligence. It is far better for the wrong candidate to turn down the job than to take it and fail. The second reason you should help with due diligence is to communicate your desire for a win-win situation that's good for the candidate and the organization.

Geno wasn't sure he wanted to leave his current job. He agreed to meet the recruiter for breakfast in his hometown. Then he agreed to meet the hiring manager. He walked out of that meeting thinking, "I could never work for that guy." But then he got sucked into the competition for the job, and after several rounds of interviews, he got the offer and accepted on the spot. During his third week on the job, he walked out of a particularly unpleasant meeting with his boss thinking he'd make a huge mistake in accepting the job. He had. That decision led to a lot of pain for Geno, his family, and the organization during the year it took to unravel the mistake.

Due diligence is designed to mitigate three risks—organizational, role, and personal:

- *Organizational:* Give candidates information about the organization and its sustainable competitive advantage—annual reports, a recent strategic plan.

- *Role:* Set up a conversation with any peers the candidate will have to work with interdependently so the candidate gets a better view of how the role fits with the organization.

- *Personal:* Share information you've gathered about the candidate— not necessarily all of it, but certainly information that highlights strengths. If you misread the candidate's strengths, he or she can correct you.

HOT TIP

Helping with due diligence is a win-win idea.

Some candidates will do due diligence and accept the offer. These people will join with more confidence than they would have had if they not done due diligence.

Islip Request   5/2/2014 1:11:00 PM

Request date:5/1/2014 10:50 PM
Request ID: 45191
Call Number:658.31 B8124
Item Barcode:

|||||||||||||||||||||||||||||||||||||
3 4 7 1   1 0 0 2 0 8 1 6 4 6

Author: Bradt, George B.
Title: Onboarding : how to get your new emplo
Enumeration:c.1Year:
Patron Name:Patrick Loftus
Patron Barcode:

|||||||||||||||||||||||||||||||||||||
2 2 6 1 1 0 0 0 5 7 0 8 4

Patron comment:

Request number:

|||||||||||||||
Route to: 4 5 1 9 1
I-Share Library:

Library Pick Up Location:

Some candidates will turn down the offer based on what they learn during their due diligence. This is a good thing for all involved—even if it doesn't feel like it at the time.

An ever-growing set of particularly astute people give our book, *The New Leader's 100-Day Action Plan,* to new employees embarking on leadership positions. The most astute give new leaders that book with their offer letters and point them toward the chapter on due diligence.

TIME-SAVER

Standard operating procedure is to try to close the sale as quickly as possible after the offer.

Certainly encouraging due diligence slows things down over the short term.

If your lead candidate turns the job offer down after doing due diligence, things are slowed down even more.

However, the time wasted in replacing someone who leaves after showing up for work so far outweighs those minor delays that encouraging due diligence is a significant time-saver over the long run.

Follow-Up Phone Calls
This one's a little tricky. You want to give candidates enough time and space to think without hounding them. On the other hand, you want them to know you are thinking about them and care about them. Use your best judgment in each situation. Generally, if you are following our one-week closing plan, you probably want to initiate at least one follow-up phone call halfway through the process.

Other Phone Calls as Appropriate
Additionally, you may want to have other people call the candidate to express their enthusiastic support for his or her joining the

organization. Think about peers or other people the candidate met while interviewing.

Other Live Meetings to Alleviate Concerns and Drive Important Messages

In many cases, another live meeting between offer and acceptance may be warranted. This is particularly true if taking the job involves a family relocation.

You, or others, may want to meet the candidate's spouse or partner directly to understand and address his or her needs, hopes, desires, and concerns.

Close the Sale

Don't forget to ask for the sale!

GUEST EXPERT

Bill Epifanio on Closing the Sale[1]

When it comes to hiring, closing the sale involves some interesting dynamics and tensions. As the employer, your role has flipped from buyer to seller. Presumably, you and your organization have done your part: you've clearly defined the role; communicated the reciprocal fit; addressed or mitigated concerns; helped with your prospect's due diligence; and, generated sincere enthusiasm. While hiring is a delicate matchmaking process, you are running a business, which can't wait indefinitely for the talent it needs. It's reasonable to expect an answer to your offer by a specific date and it's now time to manage your candidate's expectations.

Giving a candidate 24 hours to commit to your offer communicates a degree of urgency and pressure that is not appropriate in most situations. Giving a candidate a week is generally reasonable. The point is that you need a decision from the candidate on a timely enough basis for you to be able to turn to backup candidates before they lose interest. Communicating to the candidate that you'd appreciate an answer in one week, then politely requesting a reaction and commitment to the one-week response time, is absolutely appropriate.

Several pieces of advice here:

- *Applying excessive time pressure is extremely counterproductive.* It can signal desperation and adds a rug-trading element to the interaction that's probably inconsistent with your corporate style and values. Remember, if this match isn't meant to be, rushing things won't help. Worse yet, doing so can get you into a nasty employment situation that extra time could have helped you avoid.
- *Don't mention the other candidates.* While most candidates will correctly assume there are other candidates, they never appreciate being reminded of, or tacitly threatened by, their own competition. Please respect your candidate's ego. It's usually bigger than you'd like to think, especially in the case of senior executives.
- *Blame the market.* If the situation demands communicating some urgency, blame something out of your control, like pressing market demands.
- *Generally, a tactful nudge is perfectly acceptable.* Alternatively, if you are working with an executive recruiter, let the recruiter do the nudging.

Despite all efforts to standardize your organization's hiring process, the hiring experience with each candidate is both unique and telling. Almost every interaction between you and your potential hire provides you with new and valuable information—adding more detail to your picture of the candidate. How the candidate responds to your employment offer tells you a great deal, reinforcing or challenging your prior evaluations. For example:

- You believe you've been completely reasonable and accommodating regarding the candidate's due diligence requests, but more requests keep coming. You might have an overly idealistic candidate or a stylistic mismatch.
- Your firm is entrepreneurial and growth oriented, but your candidate is asking for more cash compensation versus equity or possibly other financial guarantees. You might have uncovered a fundamental cultural mismatch.
- Your candidate can't commit to your offer in what you feel is a reasonable period of time. Your candidate is demonstrating a level of indecisiveness that won't bode well for his future job performance with your organization.

Each closing process tends to evolve dynamically with a unique tone and outcome. Remember that how you handle this process will leave a lasting impression, for better or worse, on your candidate or new hire.

Make Sure the Sale Stays Closed

Strong candidates always have other options. Those options don't magically disappear the moment someone accepts a job. Make sure you understand your candidate's options. Help him or her think through (and even practice) disengagement. You absolutely must help your candidate prepare to deal with a counteroffer from the current employer. By mentally preparing to reject a counteroffer, your candidate is much less likely to be swayed.

Wang-Li thought Jane's old company would pressure her to reject his offer and stay put. So Wang-Li walked her through a practice session on how to handle a counteroffer.

What Wang-Li had not counted on was her old company putting Jane on a plane to spend an entire day with the CEO, John Doe. Even so, Jane ended up writing a nice letter to John Doe explaining her decision to accept Wang-Li's offer and join the new company.

One month after she'd started, Jane was in her office and the phone rang.

"Jane."

"This is John Doe. Do you have a few minutes to talk about the letter you wrote? I'd really value your insight so we can keep from losing good people like you in the future."

It didn't end with this. People from Jane's old company "happened" to bump into her periodically. All urged her to return. Finally after a year, she did.

Obviously, this is an extreme example of a company following through on a counteroffer. If you are not looking for people who are appreciated as much as John Doe appreciated Jane in this example, then you are not aiming high enough. It's not enough to get people like this to say yes once. You have to get them to say yes every day.

MASTER CLASS

Make training on strategic selling mandatory for *all* managers. Everybody can benefit from deliberate practice in strategic selling because everybody can do a better job of understanding others' needs, figuring out how to solve others' problems, and communicating those solutions to the people involved.

Summary and Indicated Actions

Success here is not getting more people to accept your job offers. It is getting the right people to accept your job offers for the right reasons. A strategic selling approach will lose you some sales. That's a good thing. The steps of such a strategic sale include:

1. Identify the players in the decision-making process:
   - *Economic buyer (and likely User buyer):* The decision maker— the new employee.
   - *Technical buyer:* A person who can say "no" but can't say "yes"— family members.
   - *Coach:* A person who can influence the decision.
2. Pinpoint why the organization and role are right for this candidate.
3. Spell out why you think the candidate is right for the organization and role.
4. Understand the decision maker's concerns.
5. Understand the influencers' needs, hopes, desires, and concerns.
6. Think through ways to alleviate the candidate's and influencers' concerns.
7. Develop and implement your selling campaign:
   - Verbal offer
   - Written offer
   - Help with due diligence
   - Follow-up phone calls
   - Other live meetings
   - Close the sale/targeted acceptance date
   - Make sure the sale stays closed

Focus

- *Manager:* Close the sale with the right candidate. Support the prospective employee's due diligence efforts.
- *Employee:* Do real due diligence.
- *Human Resources:* Support the hiring manager by preparing the offer and supporting selling efforts.

PART III

GIVE YOUR NEW EMPLOYEE A BIG HEAD START BEFORE DAY ONE

Co-Create a Personal Onboarding Plan with Your New Employee

Big Head Start

Total Onboarding Program (TOP)				
Align>	Acquire>	Accommodate>	Assimilate>	Accelerate>
			Day One	IV. Enable and Inspire
		III. Big Head Start Make your employee ready and able to do real work on day one (9) Manage the announcement to set new employee up for success. (8) Co-create a personal onboarding plan with your new employee. (7)		
	II. Recruit			
I. Prepare				

Getting a big head start is one of the best ways to get up to speed faster.

By the end of this chapter, your employee will have a personal onboarding plan. Because you co-create the plan, you and your new employee will be in complete agreement.

Co-creating the personal onboarding plan is a powerful demonstration of your interest in your new employee's success. People quit people before they quit organizations; so by working together in consultative cooperation to put together the plan, you invite the emotional engagement that should result in encouragement, leaving little room for regret to sneak in. In this first official interaction with your new employee, you begin leading at a most personal level.

This chapter walks you through the personal onboarding plan from start to finish. Sequence matters. Think about four phases: prework, listening, working together, and handing off.

Pre-work gives your employee information and, thus, opportunity to be knowledgeable enough to work with you as an equal player when you meet face-to-face. *Listening* warms up your interaction and gives you a heads-up on potentially important issues by allowing your new employee to present his or her thinking unencumbered by your expectations or preconceived notions. *Working together* completes the personal onboarding plan and models the cooperative relationship you hope to have when you do more real work together in the future. *Handing off* clearly delineates who does what and gives evidence of your expectation that your new employee will own his or her onboarding completely from this point forward.

A MODEL FOR INSPIRING AND ENABLING

Pre-work, listening, working together, handing off is a good model to use when thinking about not just this first personal onboarding planning meeting but how to work with your new employee under most circumstances:

- *Pre-work* sets them up for success.
- *Listening* demonstrates that you value their input.
- *Working together* helps both of you learn and grow.
- *Handing off* is an essential part of empowering.

Use the process of co-creating the plan to correct any divergence in employee and organization expectations. It's easy for new employees to feel they have mandates they don't really have, particularly when you oversold to get a candidate to say "yes." Make corrections now. Check and recheck those divergent expectations at every step of onboarding.

Pre-work—Stakeholders

Your work comes first. Download Tool 7.1 Personal Onboarding Plan from www.onboarding-tools.com. Complete the stakeholders section. To be thorough and start out well aligned, get input from your HR partner and, if appropriate, the mentor, buddy, and *touchstone* you plan to assign to your new employee. Key stakeholders are those people who can have the most impact on your new employee's success in the new role. People often fail to think through this process or look in only one direction to find stakeholders. Others make the mistake of treating everyone as a key stakeholder and end up trying to please everybody. Both of these approaches are doomed to fail.

Types of Stakeholders

Up stakeholders: May include your new employee's boss whether or not it's you, an indirect boss if there is a matrix organization, his or her boss's boss (your boss), the board of directors, or anyone else situated further *up* in the organization.

Across stakeholders: Might include allies, peers, partners, and even the person who wanted the job but didn't get it or the person moving out of the job. Across stakeholders that people often overlook include clients, customers, and suppliers (both external and internal).

Down stakeholders: Usually include your new employee's direct reports and other critical support people who are essential to successful implementation of the team's goals. Obviously, your new employee's assistant should be high on this list because he or she can often serve as an additional set of eyes and ears.

Former stakeholders: If you are promoting someone from within, make sure to take into account your new employee's *former* stakeholders—up, across, and down from the former position.

NOTE TO HR

You play an important role in helping the manager identify all stakeholders and focus on the most critical stakeholders.

Planning Meeting

Set up a 60 to 90 minute face-to-face, one-on-one planning meeting as soon after acceptance as possible. Make sure you can give your new employee and the work at hand your full attention. Consider meeting offsite to limit disruption. Your single-minded focus on your new employee and his or her personal onboarding plan is a powerful sign of how much you value that person as an individual and as an important new player on your team.

Michael invited Belinda into the office 10 days before her start date. Belinda was amazed at how Michael focused on her:

- They met in a conference room on a different floor than Michael's office so they would not be interrupted.
- Michael turned off his cell phone.
- Michael listened to her ideas and concerns without any regard to time.
- At the end of the meeting, Michael took her back to "their floor" to see her new office and decide what color she wanted on the walls, what furniture she wanted, and how she wanted the office set up—so the company could have it all in place for her when she showed up 10 days later.

Both Bill Clinton and George Bush Sr. were famous for making people feel like the only person in the room when they met with them. Michael did the same thing with Belinda. It's not hard to do. The impact is huge and enduring.

Send a meeting pre-work package that includes:

- Personal onboarding plan with stakeholders' information
- Personal onboarding plan instructions
- Job description
- Organization charts
- Other information that can inform planning

Ask your new employee to complete the pre-work as well as possible. Be clear that you will use your time together, when you meet, to revise and improve the plan. Resist giving specific direction. You want to create an opportunity for your employee to reveal his or her natural level of initiative and detail orientation.

Tool 7.1

Personal Onboarding Plan (Downloadable)

Stakeholders

Up	*Anna, Bart*
Across	*Anna, Charlie, Devon, Edgar, Fran, Gina, Hal, Meg, Norb, Oscar*
Down (Former*)	*Henry, Ingrid, Jack Jr., Kia, Larry*

Message

Platform for change	*Safety issues have compromised delivery*
Vision	*Timely, complete, safe delivery of water to operations*
Call to action	*Improve system, reduce accidents, manage process*
Headline	*Totally safe water*

Fuzzy Front End

Personal setup	*Get own pail set*
Jump-start learning	*Read manuals*

Pre-start Stakeholder Conversations

• Live:	*Jill, Jack Jr.*
• Phone:	*Charlie, Devon, Edgar, Fran, Gina, Henry, Ingrid, Kia, Larry*
Announcement Cascade	*Pivot around June 26 (pre-annc-post)*

Day One

Breakfast for group, New Manager Assimilation session with team

First Week

Meetings with Anna, Meg, Norb, Oscar, Charlie, Devon, Edgar, Fran, Gina, Henry, Ingrid, Kia, Larry

Key Events

Burning imperative (by day 30)	*Group session by end of July*
Milestones (by day 45)	*Immediately following group session*
Early wins plans (by day 60)	*Picked by Labor Day*
Team roles (by day 70)	*Decide by mid-Sept*
Communication steps	*Ongoing*

*If promoted from within

The pre-work we provide in Tool 7.1 Personal Onboarding Plan, should be self-explanatory. It sets your new employee up to act like a partner, not a subordinate, when you work together. Expect to learn something from each employee's unique perspective. You, of course, are well equipped to add value based on your onboarding planning and organizational knowledge.

If you want to offer your new employee even more help with new job planning, take a look at these resources:

- *The New Leader's 100-Day Action Plan:* A complete onboarding how-to book for executives
- www.NewJobPrep.com: An online onboarding prep work stream
- www.onboardingworkshops.com: Information about live onboarding prep workshops
- www.PrimeGenesis.com: More on executive onboarding and leadership transition acceleration

Listen

When you meet, remember your objective is to make the co-creation effort "the beginning of a beautiful relationship." Be authentic and transparent. Listen, listen, and listen. Model the behavior you want from your new employee. This is an important pivot point in your relationship.

Start your meetings by asking your new employee to share his or her thinking by presenting a personal onboarding plan. Allow him or her to structure his or her own thoughts. You will learn something about the way he or she thinks and presents. You may want to note communication skills that need improvement. Incorporate those notes in your employee development plans.

HOT TIP

If you expect your employee to inject new behavior into your team culture, you must be especially diligent and consistent about modeling that new behavior starting now. Consciously or subconsciously, your new employee *will* adapt and perform to your lead.

After listening (really listening) to your employee present his or her thinking, work through and revise the plan together. Have your employee update the plan as you go. Start at the top of the personal onboarding plan, and work down in the following sequence:

- Stakeholders
- Message
- Fuzzy front End
- Day one
- First week
- Key Events

Note: do not let your new employee initiate the "Fuzzy front end" pre-start stakeholder discussions until you complete the Announcement Cascade (Tool 8.1). Read "Speed Development of Important Working Relationships" (Chapter 11) for more observations about enabling pre-start stakeholder discussions.

I found out later that one of the directors of a different department had wanted her husband to have my position. And since he did not get it, the next five years she did everything in her means to make my position harder than it needed to be. The president was aware of the issue, but decided not to do anything about it. So having the knowledge of team players and the ones that are out to destroy you will have you heading in the right direction to begin with so that pitfalls can be avoided or at a minimum be addressed.

—PrimeGenesis Client

Hand Off the Plan

When you finish improving and revising the plan, it's time to make the handoff. Now, your new employee takes full ownership of execution of his or her own personal onboarding plan. You become the onboarding coach. Think about EASE-ing your employee's transitions into his or her new job:

- *Encourage.*
- *Align* others around the plan.
- *Solve* problems that get in the way.
- *End* distractions by helping your employee focus on what really matters and ignoring the stuff that doesn't matter.

While you EASE through getting things ready for your new employee to do real work (chapter 9) and "Speed Development of Important Working Relationships" (chapter 11), you will have many to-dos. Be accountable to your new employee. Reference the personal onboarding plan when you let your employee know where you are on tasks that support his or her onboarding. Once more—*your employee is in charge of onboarding from now on.* You are a supporting player or the stage manager. Be clear about the handoff. This is a great opportunity to learn to what degree your new employee is willing and able to take the ball and run with it. Some will do a great job. Others will need encouragement and, perhaps, skill enhancement.

That's it. Done well, your employee will walk out of this meeting certain about what's next and thinking "what a clear path; what a great boss." Mission accomplished!

TIME-SAVER

Everything about creating a tactical personal onboarding plan is a time-saver. The planning meeting jump-starts your relationship with your new employee. Just having a documented onboarding plan gives your new employee confidence to move faster.

Create an onboarding plan review board to provide managers and new employees input on personal onboarding plans. A review board supports cross-fertilization of the best ideas in personal onboarding plans while deepening the knowledge and skills of the onboarding managers and the members of the review board.

Summary and Indicated Actions

Creating an individual personal onboarding plan with your new employee is a good way to take the giant step from you and me to we. Investing the time to do this is a powerful sign of how much you value your new employee. This is as much about building your personal relationship with him or her as it is about getting the plan right. Having said that, you still want to get the plan right. We suggest the following steps:

Pre-work

- Your pre-work in identifying stakeholders, provides your new employee with information to start thinking about the plan.
- Your new employee's pre-work is a first pass at the personal onboarding plan.

Listening

- Start your first planning meeting by listening to your new employee's plan ideas. Allow employees to structure their own thoughts.

Working Together

- Truly partner to create the best possible personal onboarding plan for this employee in this organization at this point in time.

Handing Off

- Step back so the new employee can implement the plan with you EASE-ing the way behind the scenes by Encouraging, Aligning, Solving, and Ending distractions.

Focus

- *Manager:* Co-create the personal onboarding plan.
- *Employee:* Co-create the personal onboarding plan.
- *Human Resources:* Provide information and support.

Personal Onboarding Plan Instructions (for the Hiring Manager to Give to the New Employee)

Stakeholders

Stakeholders are people who are critical to your job success. Resist treating everyone as a key stakeholder, because you don't want to be spread so thin that you give inadequate attention to truly important players.

I have worked with HR to map your stakeholders for you. You have up, across, down, former, hidden, and outside stakeholders:

- *Up stakeholders* are people who hold a higher rank and are essential to your job success. Up includes me, as well as my boss.
- *Across stakeholders* include allies, peers, customers, clients, and partners—even people who wanted but did not get your job.
- *Down stakeholders* are your direct reports and critical support people.
- *Former stakeholders* are the stakeholders from your previous job if you were promoted or transferred from within the organization.
- *Hidden stakeholders* are people in the organization who have extraordinary influence beyond titles and rank.
- *Outside stakeholders* include clients and vendors.

Your *personal board* consists of stakeholders who will be most critical to your success. I have circled those individuals on your onboarding plan. Never surprise a personal board member. Give them chances to proffer informal, off-the-record advice. You should be eager for and welcome all feedback from personal board members. Over time, please work to develop deep relationships with these people.

Message

"We are what we think about." Your message is what you want people to think about. If I am a new customer service manager and my job success depends on getting my team to make customers feel good about my company, my message might be "we work for our customers." If I am a new sales manager and my job success depends on eliminating discount pricing, my message might be "we add more value with service than discounts." You get the point! Your message is your rallying cry.

To discover your message, answer the following three questions:

1. *Identify the platform for change.* What needs to happen differently? Pivot off your job description.

2. *Describe your vision of success.* When you have delivered the business results for which you were hired, what will things look like?

3. *Create a call to action.* What should people do to drive toward your vision?

Synthesize your thinking into one, simple bumper-sticker message ("We work for our customers!" "We add more value with service than discounts!"). You will use your message as a mantra. You will frame challenges with the message, start and end meetings with the message, label team successes as demonstrations of the message. Message as mantra. We are what we think about. Document your message and your thinking behind the message on your personal onboarding plan.

Personal Setup

No matter how much you try, you can't give a new job a best effort until your home life and family is comfortable. Figure out housing, schools, transportation, and so on. Now, before you show up for work, is the time to get things in motion. Use the personal setup checklist to scope out your needs. Note your most important personal setup to-dos on the onboarding plan.

Learning

Is there information about the organization or your job that you want but don't have? Document learning action items on your onboarding plan. It is not important to have learned everything before day one, but it is crucial to have a learning plan in place.

Pre-start Stakeholder Discussions

These are structured conversations between you and your stakeholders that you initiate, ideally, before day one. Everything you do communicates. This includes whom you talk to, in what forum, and in what order. People you talk to early will feel valued by you. Those scheduled late on the agenda might feel slighted. So make sure you schedule discussions with stakeholders as early as possible. The objectives of pre-start stakeholder discussions include:

- Establishing a primary relationship with each stakeholder
- Searching for different perspectives, not one truth
- Learning about individual stakeholder expectations
- Gathering knowledge about resources and "how things get done around here"
- Learning how best to communicate with each stakeholder

It is helpful to break discussions into: (1) warm-up, (2) learning, (3) expectations, and (4) implementation. The Onboarding Conversation Guide (Tool 7.2) offers a successful format. Start each discussion with an effort to understand the stakeholder's wants and needs at a personal level. Something as simple as asking "tell me about yourself" can open up communication.

During the learning part of the discussions, focus on perceptions and strengths. Perceptions have to do with understanding each stakeholder's assessment of the situation. Different stakeholders will have different views of the same situation. Some will think things are going well. Others will think things need to be turned around quickly to prevent an impending disaster. Focus on the perceptions of each individual to figure out how to interact well with that stakeholder. Stakeholders will also have different perceptions of what strengths exist in the organization and what strengths need to be developed.

Tool 7.2

Onboarding Conversation Guide (Downloadable)

Key questions to ask during onboarding conversations (in addition to the questions you
  would normally ask).

Learning

Give me your read on the general *situation*?

_____

_____

What *strengths/capabilities* are required?

_____

_____

Which strengths/capabilities exist now? Examples?

_____

_____

Expectations

What do you see as *priorities*? Lower priorities? Current untouchables?

_____

_____

What *resources* are available to invest against these priorities?

_____

_____

Implementation

Tell me about the control points (metrics and process: meetings, reports)

_____

_____

Tell me about some of the decisions we make. Who makes them? How? What?
  1. A alone 2. A w/B's input 3. Shared 4. B w/A's input 5. B alone

_____

_____

What is the best way to *communicate* with you? (Mode/manner/frequency/
  disagreements?)

_____

_____

Try to understand stakeholder views of priorities and what resources are available and required. These conversations will be different up, across, and down. Up, you will be looking for direction. Across, you will be looking to build mutual understanding. Down, you will look for current reality and needs.

At this stage in interactions with stakeholders, it is very important that you listen well but don't offer opinions. You just don't know enough yet to offer an opinion.

List the stakeholders (in order of priority) with whom you would like to have conversations before day one and during the first week or two on the job. We will review and perhaps edit your list when we meet. List who/when/how (meeting, phone call, etc.) on the personal onboarding plan. As conversations are not yet scheduled, pencil in ideal dates. You can update the plan as we schedule discussions.

HOT TIP

Pre-start stakeholder discussions can be game changing. The answers people get before day one are different from those they get after the start, because before day one new employees are perceived as just trying to make connections and learn. It is too soon for hidden agendas.

Day One

I will let you know where to be, at what time on day one. Right now, you should think through your entry strategy. The biggest choice to be made is how best to engage with the existing culture. When it comes to cultural engagement, it is helpful to think in terms of the ACES model. This model makes a very tricky subject easy. Under the ACES model there are only three cultural engagement choices: (1) **A**ssimilate, (2) **C**onverge and **E**volve, and (3) **S**hock. Note your choices with tactical details on your plan.

More Thoughts for the Hiring Manager—Key Events

- *Burning imperative:* The date by which your employee and his or her direct report team should have a co-created burning imperative in place. That date should be no more than 30 days after the new employee's start date. A burning imperative is the thing the team must achieve to accomplish target business results. Your employee's burning imperative should flow from your team's burning imperative. For more information, see *The New Leader's 100-Day Action Plan*. When the burning imperative is in place, your employee should note it on his or her onboarding plan.

- *Milestones:* The date by which your employee and his or her direct report team should have their co-created operating milestones in place. That date should be no more than 45 days after the start. Milestones are target accomplishments that, when achieved, will mark team progress toward target business results. For more, see Chapter 12 or *The New Leader's 100-Day Action Plan*. When milestones are in place, your employee should note them on the onboarding plan.

- *Early wins:* Write in the date by which your employee and his or her direct report team will have identified and laid plans for early wins. That date should be no more than 60 days after the start. Early wins are key, visible accomplishments that model exceptional performance and progress toward target business results. Early wins are milestones against which the team invests extra resources. For more, see *The New Leader's 100-Day Action Plan*. When target early wins are identified, your employee should note them on the onboarding plan.

CHAPTER 8

Manage the Announcement to Set Your New Employee Up for Success

Big Head Start

Total Onboarding Program (TOP)				
Align>	Acquire>	Accommodate>	Assimilate>	Accelerate>
			Day One	IV. Enable and Inspire
		III. Big Head Start Make your employee ready and able to do real work on day one (9) Manage the announcement to set new employee up for success. (8) Co-create a personal onboarding plan with your new employee. (7)		
	II. Recruit			
I. Prepare				

Managing the announcement is one of the most important things you can do to make your new employee feel welcome, valued by, and valuable to your organization.

Jethro, do you want me to bring Wally to the meeting?

"Wally?"

"You know, the new guy. . . . Hmm. . . . The look on your face says you don't know."

What was especially awkward about this situation was that Wally was one of Jethro's direct reports. Jethro's boss had hired Wally and assigned him to Jethro's team—without bothering to mention it to

Jethro. Jethro's boss scored a twofer, managing to make both the new employee and the new employee's boss feel bad in one fell swoop.

You are not going to fall into that trap. You are going to make sure your new employee's stakeholders across, down, and even up are ready to make your new employee feel welcome, valued, and valuable and then help him or her and the team succeed.

The basics are straightforward:

- Map the stakeholders.
- Clarify the messages.
- Lock in the timing and wording of the official announcement.
- Determine who you're going to talk to before the announcement, as well as when and how.
- Decide who you're going to talk to after the announcement, but before the new employee starts.
- Implement, track, and adjust as appropriate.

Map the Stakeholders

We talked about stakeholders in chapter 7. If you skipped that section, go back and read it now.

Clarify the Messages

There may be three messages in play at this point:

1. Your message to your new employee
2. Your message to your new employee's stakeholders
3. Your new employee's message to his or her stakeholders

However many messages there are, they must drive to the same destination. While different messages may have different platforms for change and different calls to action, they must share the same vision of the future.

You can't get people to do anything differently unless they believe that there is a reason to change (platform for change), can picture themselves in a better place (vision), and know what to do to be part of the way forward (call to action).[1]

To illustrate these points, imagine a pack of polar bears. They are playing on an ice flow. It's melting! It's drifting out to sea! The polar bears will drown or starve to death. Either scenario is not good (platform for change). The good news is that there's some ice nearby that's sitting on land with access to food. The bears could play there, be safe, and get food (vision). So, polar bears, how about swimming over to the other ice (call to action)?

Keep in mind that everyone in the organization affected by the new employee wants to know the same thing: "How will the changes this person brings impact me?" When you are crafting your communication points, make sure you: explain how the changes the new employee brings will enable other people to be more successful, and treat everyone decently as human beings.[2] Do these, and you will go a long way toward providing a motivating answer to their real question (How will the changes impact me?)

Your Message to Your New Employee

This should look a lot like the message you delivered to the new employee while you were recruiting. You do not need to emphasize a platform for change at this point because moving into a new job is enough to make almost anyone realize they are embarking on something different.

Your vision of a brighter future is the piece that should be as consistent as possible across audiences and time. The closer your vision and your new employee's vision match, the better it is for everyone involved. This vision of a brighter future will likely form the backbone of your headline or rallying cry. Get this right early on and stick with it.

The call to action will probably vary by audience. You probably want your new employee to avoid common pitfalls and get a quick start. (If not, why are you reading a book about how to get your new employees up to speed in half the time?)

Your Message to Your New Employee's Stakeholders

The lazy way out is to use the addition of the new employee as the platform for change. Don't do that. That positions the new employee as a problem to be solved as opposed to part of the solution.

Second from the bottom of the list is to position the new employee's predecessor as the reason things have to change, blaming them for any existing problems. Don't do that. It will disturb at least some of the people you are talking to, including those who thought the predecessor was doing a good job, those that liked the predecessor, and even those who agree with you but wonder what you are going to say about them when they leave.

Instead, use external change as the platform for change. Position your new employee as part of a change initiative that will improve your business. Ideally, this is the same platform for change you are using to drive change across your entire area of responsibility.

The vision you use to create your message for your new employee's stakeholders needs to be identical to what you've been driving broadly. The call to action for your new employee's stakeholders should look a lot like what you've been telling them to do ("keep moving forward with what we have in place") with the addition of a call to action to welcome the new employee and be open to the new changes to follow.

Your Employee's Message

The closer your new employee's platform for change and vision are to yours, the better. Your employee's call to action should match your stakeholder's call to action minus the bit about welcoming the newcomer. In general:

	Platform for Change	Vision	Call to Action
Manager to new employee	NA	Core vision	Avoid common pitfalls Make a quick start
Manager to key stakeholders	External change	Core vision	Keep moving forward Welcome newbie Be open to changes
New employee to key stakeholders	External change	Core vision	Keep moving forward Be open to changes

Lock in the Timing and Wording of the Official Announcement

Because you are going to build the announcement cascade off the timing of the formal announcement, set the announcement date before you take any actions to build the cascade. Map this one out to the minute, particularly if your organization operates in different time zones. For example, an announcement going out at 5 PM London time won't get seen by most people in Asia until the next day.

Work through the wording of the announcement. Your message to stakeholders will inform the main components of an announcement:

- The change we're announcing (xxx moving into yyy role)
- Why this is a good thing in general (vision)
- Why we're making a change (platform for change)
- Why we hired the new employee (employee background, strengths)
- Who else is impacted (other moves, new reporting lines)
- What people should do next (call to action)

NOTE TO HR, PUBLIC RELATIONS, OR OTHER INFLUENCERS

Help the manager think through and craft the formal announcement. Take into consideration the wide range of internal and external stakeholders that will see it, read it, or hear about it. Help the manager time the announcement. Again, consider the full range of stakeholders.

GUEST EXPERT

Jean Brown on Communication[3]

Great communicators connect, inspire, and persuade. To *connect*, you must engage your audience in the message. You should *inspire* confidence. And you have to *persuade* your listeners to action. Successful communication demands that you craft a clear, concise, persuasive message and deliver it effectively. Both components matter.

CRAFTING A CLEAR, CONCISE, PERSUASIVE MESSAGE

Language matters. As you develop your platform for change and vision, ask yourself: What is the *one* thing I want my audience to remember? They won't remember everything you say. Your goal should be this: if Joe walks out of your

(continued)

(continued)

meeting and runs into Jane, who missed it, could Joe play back your key message in one sentence?

Four keys to an effective message:

1. **Concrete:** Don't talk in vague concepts; be specific.
2. **Targeted to your audience:** What are their priorities?
3. **Pithy, memorable:** Will everyone be able to play it back?
4. **Short:** 10 words or fewer.

We can learn a lot about strong messaging from the experts—speech-writers and copywriters. Consider these examples pulled from politics and pop culture.

The most effective messages are short and simple.

I Have a Dream (Martin Luther King, Jr., 1966)

This famous speech contains, arguably, the most powerful message of any political speech in recent history. Notice that it contains four words, all one syllable.

Stay away from flowery language and jargon. This is not the time to show off your big vocabulary.

Mr. Gorbachev, Tear Down This Wall! (Ronald Reagan at the Berlin Wall, 1991)

Ronald Reagan didn't say, "Let us end the divide between communism and democracy and come together with peace and harmony throughout the world." No. He shouted "Tear down this wall"—specific, direct, actionable, short, and memorable. That wall came down.

Memorable messages give you something unexpected, as in the Adidas advertising slogan:

Impossible Is Nothing (Adidas global advertising campaign)

The slogan could easily have read: "Nothing is impossible." It means the same thing. But instead, they flipped the cliché on its head. Now your brain hears something unexpected. Your brain has to stop and process the message. That's one way ads break through the clutter and stick.

Hot Tip for Persuasive Messaging

When laying out your vision of the future—think about the benefits to your listener. Appeal to what we call the "universal motivators": money, time, and feelings.

Money

- Make money: Develop new business. Increase revenue.
- Save money: Cut costs, improve profitability.

Time

- Save time.
- Improve efficiency.

Feelings

- Build ego, power, or cachet.
- Improve morale, and so on.

    This type of benefit language will move people in your direction.

    In summary, although you are not writing ad slogans, pay attention to the language. Challenge yourself to craft a powerful key message that will move your listeners to action.

Delivering Your Message

Note to self: There are no casual presentations. At work, you are always presenting yourself to others, and they are always forming impressions of you. So be sure you are projecting yourself as you want others to see you.

    Whether you plan to communicate with your employee's stakeholders in large groups, small groups, or one-on-one meetings, you will need to project confidence and enthusiasm for your message. And you will need to know if your message is connecting. Here are some quick tips for delivering information effectively:

- **Connect.** Keep your eyes up out of your paper. It's okay to use notes, just don't talk to the notes—they are not your audience! Look your audience in the eyes as you speak. Strong eye contact projects confidence and gives you

(continued)

(continued)

credibility. Strong eye contact also enables you to gauge audience reaction to your message. Eye contact is not simply a mechanical skill of looking around the room. The skill is to look people in the eye to see how your message is being received. This understanding allows you to adapt to the moment as needed.

- **Show your enthusiasm.** When introducing your new employee to others, you are delivering a *good news* message. Your body language and tone of voice must communicate good news. So, we'd better see you smile! Use natural gestures and avoid speaking in monotone.

Determine Who You're Going to Talk to Before and After the Announcement, When and How

Different forms of communication are better for different situations. In general:

- *Mass* communication is good for informing at a surface level.
- *Large group* meetings convey more emotion and allow for some limited interaction.
- *Small group* meetings are good for discussion to build understanding and commitment.
- *Individual* meetings are important for things that emotionally impact those individuals.

Start with Those Emotionally Impacted by the Change

People who are emotionally impacted by the change are most likely going to be:

- The boss (if it's not you)
- The person the new employee will replace
- People who wanted the job the new employee is getting
- People directly reporting to the new employee
- People who report directly to the person the new employee is replacing, but who will not report to the new employee
- People who will have to work especially closely with the new employee (internally and externally)

- People who worked especially closely with the person the new employee is replacing (internally and externally)
- People whose resources or potential resources were impacted by hiring the new employee (whether or not they will have any interaction with the new employee)

Consider telling these people the news in *individual meetings* or phone calls so they can ask you their personal questions directly. (All of which are subsets of "How will the changes impact me?") Some of them may get emotional. To give them a chance to get emotional in private is the respectful thing to do. To surprise them in front of others is less considerate.

Those Directly Impacted

Then move on to people who can be told in *small groups*. The small group list is generally made up of the people you considered but did not schedule for individual meetings. These tend to be less emotionally involved people who are directly impacted by your hiring decision. You want them to understand your reasoning and to commit to helping your new employee.

Those Indirectly Impacted

Other people who were indirectly impacted can be told in *large group* meetings where they can sense your commitment to the change and can ask some limited questions.

Those Less Impacted

Those less impacted can be made aware of the change through *mass communication.* (e.g., the formal announcement.)

HOT TIP

Have one-on-one conversations with the few people most affected by the change before they hear the news from others. The key is having the conversation. What you say will be less important than your individual care and attention.

Tool 8.1

Announcement Cascade (Downloadable)

Stakeholders (Internal and External)

Emotionally impacted: *Jill (work partner), Jack Jr. (down stakeholder)*

Directly impacted: *Down reports: Hal, Ingrid, Kia, Larry, Edgar (water retriever shift supervisor), Fran (operations center shift supervisor), Charlie (head of water retrievers), Devon (head of operations center), Gina (main contact in operations center)*

External: *Meg from water company, Norb from Weather.com, Oscar from city planning*

Indirectly impacted: *Water supply personnel, operations center associates*

Less impacted: *Anna and Bart (who already know)*

Message

Platform for change: *Predecessor's accident prompted city to tighten regulations*

Headline: *Totally safe water*

Vision: *Timely, complete, safe delivery of water*

Message points: *Strengthen system; To operations: Reduce accidents*

Call to action: *Manage process, strengthen transport system, reduce accidents, manage transport process*

Pre-announcement Time Line (one-on-ones, small groups, large groups)

Prior to announcement day

One-on-One: *Jill, Jack Jr., Charlie, Devon*
Delilah to meet with Jill and Jack Jr. prior to announcement day

Announcement day:

One-on-One: *AM phone calls with Meg, Norb, and Oscar*
Small Groups: *Water managers*

Formal Announcement

Method: _____ *live announcement* _____

Timing: _____ *June 26, noon* _____

Post-announcement Time Line (one-on-ones, small groups, large groups, mass)

One-on-One: *Calls to Meg, Norb, and Oscar*

Small Groups: *N.A.*

Large Groups: *N.A.*

Timing

Now that you've got people sorted into individual meetings, small and large group meetings, and mass communication, you can work through your timing.

A DOSE OF REALITY

News will leak. It's not that people won't try to keep secrets, if you ask them to. It's that people leak information inadvertently—e-mails open on computer screens, papers left on desks, overheard conversations, and so on.

Given that the news will start to leak as soon as you tell anyone, you should manage the cascade to maximize the chances of people hearing the news from the people you want them to hear the news from in the order that you want them to hear the news. Tool 8.1 will help you map your plan.

Think about the following phases based on a 24-hour window around the announcement itself:

Pre-window	Start of window	Announcement	End of window	Post-window
one-on-ones with key people	one-on-ones small groups	mass-media announcement	small groups one-on-ones	large group

The thinking behind this is to:

- Have the most emotionally charged conversations one-on-one in advance of the announcement window.
- Have slightly less emotionally charged conversations at the beginning of the 24-hour window (e.g., the morning before a noon announcement).
- Have small group meetings with people directly impacted right before the announcement itself so these people hear it from you, but don't have time to leak the news very far (e.g., 11 AM before a noon announcement).
- Cascade the news before the announcement, letting some of the people you told tell others in one-on-one meetings or small group meetings as appropriate.

- Have small group meetings with others indirectly impacted right after the announcement.

- Have one-on-one conversations after the announcement with people who were more emotional than expected.

- Follow up with large group meetings, further mass announcements, notes, small group meetings, and one-on-one meetings as appropriate after the announcement.

TIME-SAVER

Announcing new employees is standard operating procedure in most cases.

The problem is those announcements are often late and are generally delivered through mass communication.

The time saving idea is to cascade the announcement. It's the right thing to do for those emotionally impacted and directly impacted and will make it easier for many to absorb the news step-by-step instead of all at once.

Pre-Boarding Conversations

The pre-boarding conversation schedule must be coordinated with the announcement cascade. You may want some of the conversations to happen before the announcement, some to happen after the announcement but before the employee starts, and some to happen after the employee starts.

You will decide timing based on how closely the new employee will need to work with each individual.

If there's a critical interdependent working relationship between the employee and another individual, you want to do everything you can to nurture that relationship. So set up a pre-boarding conversation in advance of the announcement cascade. Individuals with critical working relationships with the new employee will be "in the know," and they will have met and talked to the new employee before anyone else.

In the case of slightly less critical working relationships, it probably makes sense to set up pre-boarding conversations for the time between the announcement and day one. This way the individuals can start to get to know each other before they start working together.

Everybody else can participate in individual or group onboarding conversations after the employee starts.

Implement, Track, and Adjust

About the only thing you can be sure of is that the actual cascade will not play out exactly as you had planned. This is why it's important to track the news cascade as much as possible and adjust along the way. Be ready to move up some conversations that you thought were going to happen later. Be ready for some people to have heard the news even before you get to them.

NOTE TO HR

You've got a dual role here: manage the distribution of the formal announcement and serve as eyes and ears for the manager. Pay attention to how the cascade is going. Help the hiring manager adjust.

MASTER CLASS

Run announcement cascade plans past the onboarding plan review board to further cross-fertilization of the best ideas in announcement cascades while deepening the knowledge and skills of the onboarding managers and the members of the review board.

Summary and Indicated Actions

Most managers know enough to announce new employees. Most managers don't appreciate how much that announcement will affect those emotionally impacted and directly impacted. Keep that in mind as you follow these eight steps:

1. Manage the announcement cascade in a way that sets your new employee up for success.
2. Make sure your new employee's stakeholders across, down, and up are ready to make your new employee feel welcome, valued, and valuable, and then help him or her and the team succeed.
3. Map the stakeholders (up, across, down; internal and external; emotionally impacted, directly impacted, indirectly impacted, and less impacted).
4. Clarify the messages (you to new employee, you to stakeholders, new employee to stakeholders).
5. Lock in the timing and wording of the official announcement.
6. Determine who you're going to talk to before the announcement, when and how (one-on-one, small and large groups, mass communication).
7. Decide who you're going to talk to after the announcement, but before the new employee starts.
8. Implement, track, and adjust as appropriate.

Focus

- *Manager:* Clarify and deliver messages; set up new employee's conversations.
- *Employee:* Conduct appropriate pre-boarding conversations with stakeholders.
- *Human Resources:* Manage implementation of announcement.

Do What It Takes to Make Your New Employee Ready, Eager, and Able to Do Real Work on Day One

Big Head Start

Total Onboarding Program (TOP)				
Align>	Acquire>	Accommodate>	Assimilate>	Accelerate>
		Day One	IV. Enable and Inspire	
		III. Big Head Start Make your employee ready and able to do real work on day one (9) Manage the announcement to set new employee up for success. (8) Co-create a personal onboarding plan with your new employee. (7)		
	II. Recruit			
I. Prepare				

Design your new employee's experience as you would a customer experience. People don't always remember what others said or did. They always remember how they felt.

He wanted to send the right signals on his first day. So he went over to the training building.

"Good morning."

"May I see your ID card?"

"They haven't given me one yet. I just want to look around."

"Not going to happen. No one gets in without an ID. Not even the CEO."

"I am the CEO."

No one at IBM thought to give the new CEO, Lou Gerstner, an ID card on his first day. He was unable to get into the training building. Not very accommodating. The point is not that you should make sure your new CEO can do work on day one. The point is that you should make sure all of your new employees can do real work on day one.

Accommodation

Accommodation is about getting things done, the logistics that need to be covered to make your new employee productive from the start. Do as much as you can before day one. Help your new employee complete the personal and family setup necessary to a smooth job transition so that he or she is ready, eager, and able to do real work right away. Most of accommodation is transactional, so you should focus on being efficient and thorough. However, you should always check to make sure each event that touches your new employee gets executed on message. Delegate accommodation tasks to a reliable person on your team who acts with accountability and will interface well with you, your new employee, and your human resources department.

The smallest things can make big impressions on new employees. Think about it. New employees tend to be hyperalert because they have plunged into an unknown environment. But they are completely without the institutional knowledge that established players use to navigate work life. New employees don't know "how things are done around here." That can make even simple things feel difficult. Because everything communicates, and you want to communicate your organization's focus on *real work*, clear out as many accommodation tasks as you can before day one. To get your new employees up to speed in half the time, day one and week one need to be about real work, not administrative to-dos.

Tool 9.1 Accommodation Checklist is your master document to help you do what it takes to make your new employee ready, eager, and able to do real work on day one.

Tool 9.1
Accommodation Checklist (Downloadable)

Personal Setup

___ Housing

___ Schools

___ Spousal assistance

___ Special needs

___ Cars

___ Service providers (doctors, dentists, banking, etc.)

___ Directory/reviews of local services (stores, hospitals, transportation, etc.)

___ Moving company/move assistance

___ Driver's license ___ Visas ___ Language/clture training

Work Setup

Office

___ Office/work area

___ Computer ___ Network username/password ___ Laptop

___ Phone# ___ Voice mail ___ Cell/#

___ Employee# ___ Security pass ___ Keys ___ Parking

___ Business cards ___ Personalized stationery ___ E-mail signature

___ General office supplies

___ Assistant

Information

___ Where to go for information (intranet, bulletin boards, etc.)

___ Organization history

___ Business plans

___ Financials

___ Organizational charts

___ Job descriptions and appraisals of direct reports

(*continued*)

Tool 9.1 (continued)
Accommodation Checklist (Downloadable)

___ Organization directory with names, photos, job titles, contact information

___ Facility addresses, contacts, travel directions

___ Glossary of organization specific terms

___ Customers ___ Collaborators ___ Capabilities ___ Competitors ___ Conditions

Transition Assistance

___ Spotlight profile on intranet, other open-access locations

___ Orientation

___ ''How we do things around here'' buddy

___ Mentor/coach or ___Transition accelerator

This form may be downloaded from www.onboarding-tools.com, customized, and reproduced for personal use and for small-scale consulting and training (not to exceed 100 copies per page, per year). Further use requires permission.

© 2009 PrimeGenesis LLC—All Rights Reserved | www.primegenesis.com

TIME-SAVER

Accommodation is one of the main steps of onboarding and a core plank of getting new employees up to speed. Don't waste time having the new employee show up for work if you aren't going to ensure that they will be ready to work.

Clarify Accommodation Needs and Expectations

Before you plow ahead to cover accommodation, ask your onboarding employee what he or she needs. Add requested action items to your list. Younger employees, for instance, tend to start work with more information, better technical skills, and expectations of on-demand communication. Their accommodation priorities may surprise you!

Post Information in an Easily Accessible Place

When you and your organization mobilize to accommodate new employees before day one, many people will want to know who the onboarding employee is. "How do you spell his name?" "Where is she coming from?" "What is his area of expertise?" Create an easily accessible reference by posting a spotlight about your new employee on the company intranet or somewhere else that people in your organization look for information (bulletin boards, etc.). Keep the posting very simple—just enough who/what/when information to offer confirmation and basic facts. Once on the job, your new employee can create personal profile pages on the intranet or whatever communication platforms your organization uses.

TIME-SAVER

Posting information about the new employee makes it easier for others to connect with and help that new employee.

Share Your Onboarding Plan

Make sure the people in your organization with whom your new employee will have direct contact during accommodation understand at least the spirit of your onboarding approach. If, for instance, your onboarding approach is premised on the belief that all questions are good questions, don't let people in your organization tarnish your new employee's impressions by expressing impatience. Your new employee will experience many touch points in your organization, starting with whomever he or she encounters in the parking lot on the morning of day one. The more informed and consistent the touch points, the more confidence inspiring the new job experience. So share your big picture onboarding plan.

Prepare an Appropriate Work Area

What's more unwelcoming than arriving at a new job to a disorganized work area or, worse, no work area at all? You wouldn't treat an honored guest that way. You wouldn't treat a higher-ranking member of your organization that way. Don't treat your new employee that way. Communicate how much you value your new employee by being thoughtful about his or her work setup.

A welcoming work area doesn't magically appear. An impeccable, appropriate work area only happens when someone takes personal responsibility for making sure space is created, set up, and ready according to plan. You absolutely do not want to leave office setup to your new employee. What kind of message does it send to have a new employee fussing with office setup the first week on the job? It certainly doesn't communicate the importance of focus on the work. Nor do you want to put your new employee in a position to have to try to fully engage in the work, despite an unsuitable environment.

Start by getting your new employee's input on how they like to work and what messages they want their workspace to communicate. The mere fact that you asked will impress most new employees and reinforce your personal leadership. Assign workspace setup to someone on your team or in your organization's human resources department. Give that person clear directions and accountability (what/when/at what cost). Tool 9.1 will help.

SIGNS AND SYMBOLS

Preparing an appropriate work area seems basic. It's shocking how often such a simple accommodation is neglected. Preparing an appropriate work area is the low-hanging fruit of successful accommodation.

Complete Administrative and Technical Setup Before Day One

When you hire a new employee, you have a lot to get done: compliance, federal tax forms, state tax forms, health insurance, sign-up for other company programs, review of policies and procedures, and so on. Hopefully you have a professional human resources department to handle process and paperwork. If you are on your own, just be diligent about getting it done as quickly and efficiently as possible. Don't procrastinate.

TIME-SAVER

The more administrative things you can get out of the way before day one, the more time the new employee will have to spend on building relationships and learning about the business.

Consider Using an Online Onboarding Portal

Pre-start online planning systems are now widely available. According to a 2007 survey by Towers Perrin, 18 percent of private sector employers used online tools prior to start date. Twenty-one percent plan to implement in 2008, another 21 percent in 2009.[1] Expect pre-start online planning tools to be part of new hire standard operating procedure.

TIME-SAVER

Online onboarding portals are time-savers for new employees and people already in your organization. The more administrative things you can automate, the better.

HOT TIP

Restrict use of online functions to administration and logistics. Remember, leadership is personal, and everything communicates. Nothing sends a more powerful message to your new employee than focused face time.

If you choose to use an onboarding portal, make sure you find a way to move your new employee away from the onboarding portal to your ongoing strategic employee communications platforms/channels as soon as possible. The whole point of onboarding is to get your new employee up to speed more effectively and efficiently. Don't clog the wheels by immersing your new employee in a portal that should be temporary and transactional. If possible, integrate the onboarding portal with your ongoing employee communications platform, the company's intranet, employee and benefits self-service program, and potentially others.

Sun Microsystems seems to have a good approach to this with their interactive learning environment.

GUEST EXPERT

George Selix on an Interactive Learning Environment[2]

George Selix of Sun Microsystems is in the process of building an interactive learning environment that taps into learning, books, videos, blogs, and third-party resources. The original system was built to aid enculturation, but they've gone beyond that to drive interactions between manager and employee over the first year. Some key pieces include:

- Cultural conversations (e-mails and video clips about Sun)
- Compliance learning
- Productivity tools (and hints)
- Performance management (hints)
- Strategy development aids (including a strategy simulator)
- Budgeting
- Interventions timed with key corporate milestone events

"The one piece that we're focused on is enculturation. The thing that we're trying to do is wrap our arms around our new hires and let them know that we're there for them emotionally and structurally over their first year.

"We generally get them through the first week without issue. But then things happen after that. And we need to help them.

"For example, we need to drop in a little bit of instruction in an e-mail around their first budget meeting, coupled with links to ways to learn more. Instead of making people search for it, we give it to them. Of course their boss and peers will help them, but we want to give them more.

"We've got the philosophy in place.

"Building it out, piece by piece."

Get an Assistant Settled and in Place

Put support staff in place before day one. If a new employee will have an assistant, have him or her settled and in place in advance of your new employee's arrival. It can be extremely beneficial to your new employee to have an assistant who knows the organization, particularly one who is universally well regarded. We've all experienced the positive power of a well-connected if not necessarily high-ranking ally. Alternatively, you can make temporary accommodations, if you want your new employee to have the opportunity to select his or her own assistant. In any event, if your new employee is slated to have an assistant, get someone competent settled in the role before day one so your new employee can focus on the work for which you hired him or her. Getting new employees up to speed in half the time requires a strong platform for productivity.

TIME-SAVER

This one's all about leverage. The more things support staff can take off the new employee's plate, the more time he or she can focus on areas where he or she can make higher-impact contributions.

Line Up a Mentor, Coach, or Transition Accelerator

Will your new employee have a mentor, coach, transition accelerator, or HR partner to help navigate the existing culture in the early days? Get advice from your HR partner. Present candidates to your new

Tools for the Task

Mentoring	Coaching	Transition Acceleration
Generally internal and informal	Personal advice and counsel for *new employee*	Experience-based help for *team* across key tasks
Knowledge Sharing	**Personal Development**	**Jump-start Team Performance**

Where:	On the job	Behind the scenes	In the room, with team
What	Network access	Advice & counsel	Team acceleration
Basis:	Company knowledge	Process knowledge	Operational experience
When:	**Stable situation**	**Mixed situation**	**Hot Landing**
	Time to learn	Balance learn/act	Acute need to act

employee. Make a selection based on his or her feedback. If you need help sourcing external coaches or transition accelerators, contact us through www.onboarding-tools.com.

Today's job transitions are more rapid, unsettling, and varied than ever. The good news is that there is an increased array of helpful tools and resources as depicted in the next chart.

The more complex the situation and the more urgent the transition, the more intrusive assistance should be. Internal mentors are the least intrusive, and appropriate when the only thing the new employee needs is on-the-job knowledge sharing. The next step up is transition coaching where behind-the-scenes personal development is useful. In those few, most complex situations, hands-on, operationally experienced transition accelerators may be necessary.

WHAT KIND OF HELP DOES YOUR NEW EMPLOYEE NEED?

Different situations call for different kinds of transition help. Figure out what you need, then source the best help available:

- **Mentor:** The original Mentor was a character in Homer's *The Odyssey*. When King Odysseus left Ithaca to fight the Trojan War, he entrusted the care of his kingdom and his son to Mentor. In a business context, a mentor is a more experienced individual who guides an executive's development. Mentoring is the right choice when the only thing you need is on-the-job knowledge sharing and help navigating relationships.

- **Coach:** Coaching is behind-the-scenes leadership development that tends to focus on helping individuals in their current jobs. Coaching can be the best way to address performance issues, difficult work relationships, and/or work-life balance issues. It is a way to support high-performers one-on-one through challenging organizational changes or other transitions.

- **Transition acceleration:** In complex situations, where hands-on operationally experienced help is necessary to help an executive quickly adjust to shifts in role, culture, or strategy, transition acceleration is the right help.

Here's an analogy. Professional golfers have coaches and caddies. The coaches are behind-the-scenes advisors between tournaments. The caddies, like harbor pilots and mountain climbing Sherpas, advise and counsel, but their real value is in their tangible contributions on the field of play. Where mentors and coaches work with individual executives, transition accelerators engage the full business team.

Mentoring is generally internal and informal. You may choose to mentor your new employees yourself. Or it may be better to connect them with another leader who can mentor them. Because the primary tasks of mentoring are knowledge sharing and network access, the mentor needs to understand the formal and informal workings of the organization and be able to connect the new employees with the right people.

Mentoring generally takes place on the job and is appropriate for relatively stable situations where a new employee can take time to learn and assimilate into the organization.

Emily joined the company to take over from a retiring manager. Things were going well in the group, and the organization wanted as little disruption as possible. The good news was that Emily was able to start three months before the current manager retired. The retiring manager used a large portion of the three months of overlap to mentor Emily, teaching her "the way things were done around here," introducing her to people both inside and outside the organization. As a result, by the time the manager retired, Emily was fully up to speed and doing well.

Coaching is a way for new employees to get extra personal advice and counsel. You may serve as the new employee's coach yourself and/ or you may invite others to serve that role with you or without you. Often HR generalists or peers can serve as good coaches if they understand the coaching process.

Coaching generally takes place behind the scenes and is appropriate for mixed situations where the new employee needs to learn and act at the same time.

Norman got promoted to head up packaging. He'd been in the organization and had been doing well. He'd been designated as one of the companies rising stars, and the packaging assignment was a developmental assignment for him designed to give him exposure to managing outside suppliers. The company assigned Gena to work with him as a peer coach. Gena was in charge of product supply and had extensive experience managing outside suppliers, including the packaging suppliers, so she was able to help Norman build his knowledge and skills without getting in his way.

Transition acceleration is appropriate for those few situations where the new employee must assimilate into the team and accelerate the team's transformation at the same time. These are hot landings where there is an acute need for the team to act differently, quickly.

For these situations, you will need to give your new employee the extra leverage that transition accelerators can provide. This work is generally done in the room, with the team and requires outsiders with strong operational experience.

A $1 billion-per-annum company had completely failed to implement a cross-plant information sharing system. They pulled a disparate group of people together to form a task force and appointed Anne to head it up and fix the problem fast. We helped Anne and her team move through a multistep process:

1. First the team crafted its mission, vision, objectives, goals, strategies, and plans.
2. Then the team took those plans to about a dozen stakeholders and got their input.
3. Armed with that input, the team revised their strategies and plans.
4. Then the team took the whole package to six division presidents and got their input.
5. Finally the team got the CEO's agreement and successfully implemented the plans.

What was extraordinary about this was not so much the process as the speed. From the moment the team first came together (literally, "Hi. Nice to meet you."), through all the iterations, to the moment the CEO gave final approval was 30 hours. The first team meeting was 8:30 AM on a Wednesday. The CEO approved at 2:30 PM the next day. This happened because Anne leveraged the operational experience of outsiders to cut through a lot of fuzzy areas, get to the key points, and accelerate decisions.

NOTE TO HR

In many cases, you are going to have a more clear understanding of whether the situation calls for a mentor, coach, or transition accelerator. It's important for you to help the manager understand the options and get the new employee the most appropriate resources.

TIME-SAVER

Mentors, coaches, or transition accelerators can make a huge difference in some situations.

Push New Employees to Complete Personal Setup Before Day One

No matter how hard an individual tries, he or she can't give the new job a best effort until home and family are settled. Communicate your expectation that personal setup before day one is not optional, it is a business imperative. Give the "Personal Setup" part of Tool 9.1 to your new employee to help him or her organize and complete personal setup. If employees don't cover personal setup during the "fuzzy front end," they will be distracted just when they need to be acutely aware of making positive first and lasting impressions. The first 100 days are critical. Don't let anything take your new employee's eye off the ball.

TIME-SAVER

The basic concept here is that distractions are bad. Instead of ignoring the sources of stress in your new employee's life, help and/or require him or her find expeditious solutions.

We all benefit when we have a settled place to go home to recharge at the end of the workday and on weekends. Moving and starting a new job are two of the most stressful things that can happen to an individual and his or her family, so encourage your new employee to avoid overlapping personal transitions with job transitions.

MOST STRESSFUL LIFE EVENTS

Life Event	Score
Death of spouse	100
Divorce	73
Marital separation from mate	65
Detention in jail, other institution	63
Death of a close family member	63
Major personal injury or illness	53
Marriage	50
Fired from work	47
Marital reconciliation	45
Retirement	45
Major change in the health/behavior of a family member	44
Pregnancy	40
Sexual difficulties	39
Gaining a new family member	39
Major business readjustment	39
Major change in financial status	38

Death of close friend	37
Change to different line of work	36
Major change in the number of arguments with spouse	35
Taking out a mortgage or loan for a major purchase	31
Foreclosure on a mortgage or loan	30
Major change in responsibilities at work	29
Son or daughter leaving home	29
Trouble with in-laws	29
Outstanding personal achievement	28
Spouse beginning or ceasing to work outside the home	26
Beginning or ceasing formal schooling	26
Major change in living conditions	25
Revision of personal habits	24
Trouble with boss	23
Major change in working hours or conditions	20
Change in residence	20
Change to a new school	20
Major change in usual type and/or amount of recreation	19
Major change in church activities	19
Major change in social activities	18
Taking out a mortgage or loan for a lesser purchase	17
Major change in sleeping habits	16
Major change in the number of family get-togethers	15
Major change in eating habits	15
Vacation	13
Christmas season	12
Minor violations of the law	11

Source: Holmes-Rahe Social Readjustment Scale.[3]

MASTER CLASS

Systematize accommodation so you don't have to reinvent it every time. Accommodation is one of those areas where being "good enough," cost effectively, is all you need. Spend your time creating superior knowledge and skills in other areas.

Summary and Indicated Actions

Accommodating has two parts: accommodating new employee's work needs and accommodating their personal needs. You must do both to enable them to do work. Getting this right builds your personal relationship with the new employee. Everything that goes wrong damages that relationship in one way or another. This is why it's worth investing time to make sure things are done right. Key steps:

1. Ask new employees about their needs and expectations.
2. Post information about new employees where others can find it—and then welcome them.
3. Share your onboarding plan with people who will interact with your new employee.
4. Prepare the work area.
5. Get as much as possible of the administrative and technical setup done in advance.
6. Consider an online onboarding portal for forms and information.
7. Get an assistant settled and in place.
8. Line up a mentor, coach, or transition accelerator as appropriate.
9. Push your new employee to complete his or her personal setup before day one.
10. Check in with new employees periodically along the way.

Focus

- *Manager:* Complete accommodation to-dos before day one, so day one can be about the real work.
- *Employee:* Clarify your needs and expectations. Get a head start on personal setup so personal transitions don't overlap with work transitions.
- *Human Resources:* Manage implementation of accommodation activities.

PART IV

ENABLE AND INSPIRE YOUR NEW EMPLOYEE TO DELIVER BETTER RESULTS FASTER

CHAPTER 10

Make Positive First Impressions Both Ways

Enable and Inspire

Total Onboarding Program (TOP)				
Align>	Acquire>	Accommodate>	Assimilate>	Accelerate>
			Day One	**IV. Enable and Inspire** Resources, support, follow-through. (12) Speed important working relationships. (11) Make positive first impressions both ways. (10)
		III. Big Head Start		
	II. Recruit			
I. Prepare				

Your new employee is the lead player on day one, but you are the director.

Showtime

First impressions last. Goods one confer a benefit-of-the-doubt advantage going forward. Bad ones seed questioning for a very long time. Consider day one showtime. It's your big chance to help your new employee and your organization get off to a winning start in this important relationship.

You have two constituencies to think about when planning day one. Your first constituency is your organization. On day one your new employee will make his or her first solo organization-wide impression. How will people react? Your new employee will have made a great impression on your organization if, at the end of the day, everyone is talking about how you made absolutely the right hire.

Your second constituency is your new employee. Day one will be the first, official opportunity for him or her to experience broad, unmanaged contact with your organization. This could be a warts-and-all encounter that triggers concerns, or a perfect validation of the high expectations you created during recruitment. Your organization will have made a great impression if your new employee feels the new job is exactly the opportunity he or she expected, or better.

Facilitate day one with an eye on both constituencies to achieve the positive and true first impressions *both ways* that will smooth new employee assimilation and accelerate getting up to speed. Without the shield of recruiting protocol, new employees and organizations are apt to experience a deluge of impressions and feelings. Steady everyone through the change by demonstrating your personal certainty about and commitment to your onboarding employee. Plan day one with meticulous care to leave as little to chance as possible. Mind the details of anything and everything that affects people's thoughts and feelings. Resist designing day one around operational convenience. Your ability to drive toward positive first impressions both ways will come from your ability to shake off familiarity and imagine the impact each day-one encounter will have.

Constituency 1: Your Organization

Help your new employee make a positive and true first impression.

Allow your new employee to lead the charge on day one. This is his or her first solo flight. Your job is to inspire and enable.

Scout Ahead

Do give your new employee a heads-up on the basics: what time to arrive, where to park, what to wear, and what to bring. No pop quizzes on day one, please. Make sure you know everything HR and other internal groups will need from your employee. Enable him or her to walk in with confidence by scouting ahead.

Your perspective is broad. Assemble a list for the hiring manager of all the things people will need from/expect from the new employee on day one.

TIME-SAVER

So much is new for new employees. Don't assume they know anything. Don't waste time by permitting any sink-or-swim behavior.

Anticipate the Reactions Your New Employee Will Invite

There is no template for how to plan and execute day one because success will be all about messages received, not those delivered. However, you can give your new employee a leg up by anticipating the impressions people will receive from your new employee's actions and communications. Share your experience with specific individual's perspectives and filters. Find message themes that will make it through the interpretive morass intact.

You know the personalities and predispositions. Offer your insight to the hiring manager. Encourage open-mindedness.

Help your onboarding employee give careful consideration to the three things that always hold true:

1. *Order counts.* Observers will assume that the order in which your new employee meets and communicates with people reveals who and what your new employee (or you) value. No winging it here. Help your onboarding employee do things in an order that communicates what he or she wants to communicate.

2. *Location counts.* Help your new employee figure out where he or she should be when on day one. Some things are best managed on home turf. Some interactions take on new meaning when you go out of your way to meet on someone else's turf. If your onboarding employee's job success depends on a constituency located in another department or outside of the company, part of day one should probably be spent there with them.

   A rapidly growing Internet retailer employed a VP of marketing to take the company to the next level. As the company's product was very high end, customer service had always reported to the CEO, who was also an owner. The CEO assured the new VP of marketing that he would, of course, direct customer service in all areas related to marketing. The new VP identified complaint resolution as an important marketing opportunity. However, he neglected to set foot in the call center on day one, or within the first week, much to his later regret. Location counts.

3. *Signs and symbols count.* Everything a person says/doesn't say, does/doesn't do communicates. Help your onboarding employee make deliberate choices.

DAY-ONE SIGNS AND SYMBOLS WE LIKE

Your new employee can demonstrate that he or she is an open, accessible, aboveboard player by

- Hosting a relaxed, unstructured meet and greet (early morning coffee, end of day get-together)
- Scheduling a New Leader's Assimilation session to answer questions in a structured way all at the same time

- Spending time in other departments
- Making customer visits

Expectations are heightened on the first day of anything. That's why an opening night is so exciting (and often a self-fulfilling prophecy for the full run). When you bring people onboard, everyone will be waiting to get a firsthand glimpse and to reach some early conclusions. If your hiring decision was in any way controversial, some people may even be alert to missteps or perceived flaws. Help your new employee eliminate the need to defend by leading from an offensive position from the start.

Leading? What if your new employee is not a leader; what if there isn't a direct report team? We believe every employee is a leader, because everyone in an organization needs to lead people with whom they are interdependent in order to get work accomplished. For people in roles with no direct reports, there is no better time than day one to establish the precedent of leading groups (up, down, and across) with carefully deployed personal influence.

HURDLE

Controversial New Employee

- **Problem:** Your new employee is controversial. Some aren't sure why you created the position in the first place. Others don't understand why you picked this particular person.
- **Solution:** Divide the group into supporters, detractors, and watchers. Try to move everybody one step. Give the supporters leading roles in helping the new employee and winning over the watchers. Find ways to neutralize the detractors—at least long enough to let the new employee prove him- or herself.

Direct Day-One Experiences That Support Your Employee's Messages

Experiences drive how people form opinions, relate to each other, and make sense of the world. Help your new employee design day one experiences that till the soil for the messages he or she articulated when you co-created the personal onboarding plan (chapter 7). People tend to have a receptive disposition at the beginning of periods of positive change, so day one is a great time to start seeding messages. Just seed. No stakes in the ground, yet.

On day one, your new employee should play for a tie with his or her words and move things forward with his or her actions. Trying to verbally communicate a prepared message on the first day of a new job generally doesn't work. The new employee is so clueless about the culture that the risk of saying something that means one thing to the new employee and something else to the group is very high. But acting in a way that models the future can work wonders.

Naomi's new role was primarily about helping the organization deal with local environmental regulations. She processed paperwork to get permits for transporting hazardous materials. Her message was all about partnerships—partnership with operating groups and partnership with local authorities. She came in day one, met internal stakeholders, and then took a local municipal environmental regulator to lunch. This sent a powerful signal to people in the organization that she was going to behave differently. And it sent a signal to the regulator (who greatly enjoyed lunch and, not surprisingly, insisted on paying his own way).

TIME-SAVER

The better a new employee's first impressions on others are, the less time they will have to spend correcting bad impressions and searching for common ground.

Constituency 2: Your New Employee

Make your organization impressive to your new employee.

Reality Check—Know the Impression Your Organization Will Make

Your onboarding employee is ready to start, but is your organization ready to receive? Be honest. What do you think a newcomer really sees and experiences during a first encounter? Does the question make you uncomfortable? Or are you feeling pretty proud right now?

When we are close to an organization or situation, our ability to see it like a newcomer is distorted by our own positive and negative experiences. Exposure always dulls the senses. Even if we could be truly objective, we can't reach the heightened emotional state of perception of a newcomer. The onboarding track record (Tool 2.2) that you completed in chapter 2 is a good starting point, but probably not enough.

To gain more insight into the primary experience of a newcomer to your organization, find someone with fresh eyes to be your interpreter. Designing a superlative new employee experience is much like designing a customer-centric experience. You design from the newcomer's perspective and needs, not according to your internal operating procedures. Ask an unbiased outsider (someone from a different division, a friend, a spouse . . .) to walk through day one kinds of experiences and report back to you. Be sure to ask for feelings, not just what he or she saw or heard or smelled (although sights, sounds and smells do trigger feelings).

Don't tell anyone that your interpreter will be visiting. You will want each experience—finding the parking lot, entering reception, using the restrooms, soliciting help—to be uncensored. If your interpreter is demographically similar to your new employee, all the better. Use Tool 10.1 Pseudonewcomer Audit to document your interpreter's experiences and feelings, his or her insights into expectations, emotional peaks and valleys, perceptions, and conclusions as events unfolded. Pay particular attention to your interpreter's reactions to individuals who will make your organization's first impressions. Opportunities for improvement will start to crystallize.

Design a Superlative New Employee Day-One Experience

What kind of an impression do you want your organization to make on an honored guest or a really important customer? Surely you want

Tool 10.1

Pseudonewcomer Audit
(Downloadable)

Auditor: *Mary G*
New job: *Water supply associate*
New supervisor: *Jill*
Day One: *March 1*

Who greeted: *No one ready for me. Found my way to HR*
How greeted: *New employee paperwork not ready; but they found some forms that worked.*
Where greeted: *In the HR office.*
Entrance signs and symbols: *None*
Feelings on entry: *A little neglected. But it's a big company, and I'm a small player, so it's OK.*

Welcome signs and symbols in work area: *None.*
Points made in introducing them to others: *Introduced me as a new water resource manager; that was right*
Day one activities: *Jill showed me how to do the job and put me to work. She was friendly, welcoming, concerned, and helpful.*
Feelings during the day: *It felt like the organization is very task focused. So I put my head down and did the work. It feels like a fine group to work with–once I get to know them over time. It would have been nice if more of them had introduced themselves to me. Apparently there was a bad accident recently. People seem overly cautious.*

Day one close out and take homes (for supporters at home): *None. Jill had left early for personal reasons.*
Feelings at end: *Jill was terrific during the time I spent with her. I got the feeling she'd be a wonderful person to work with. If I didn't have this audit page, I never would have expected pre-start letters, greetings, signs and symbols, close-out sessions or take homes. There was nothing wrong with my greetings. Just seems like some big opportunities to make me feel more welcome, valuable, and valued with more interactions. When asked at home how my day went, I said "About as expected. It's a job."*

---

nothing less for your new employee who, you hope, will be a highly engaged long-term member of your team. Of course you do!

Your reality check clued you in to what is. Now design the onboarding employee day one experience you want. Envision a superlative day one just as if you were designing a peak customer experience. Most new employees decide whether they will stay or go within the first six months of employment.[1] Build engagement from the start to counter those odds.

Your new employee will be hyperalert as he or she gets a first real look inside the organization to which he or she committed—so many new people, new ways of doing things, places with which to become familiar. Your day-one action plan should be as meticulous as your new employee's heightened awareness.

Every Day Is Day One

A tour of Disney's Magic Kingdom with the head groundskeeper an hour before opening gives you a glimpse into part of what makes it magical. Here's what you'd learn: The high concept of the park is "Disney movies brought to life." The different areas of the park are different scenes from different movies.

Disney leverages all the senses to set the scenes:

- *Sight:* Architecture, costumes, activities, props, and foliage
- *Hearing:* Music and background noises
- *Smell:* Smells from the restaurants, shops, and foliage
- *Taste:* Food in restaurants and snack carts
- *Feel:* Paths and surroundings

The stage management high concept is "every guest's experience should be of the same standard as what they would have experienced on the opening day of the park." It is fair to describe Disney's cast as fanatical about this. In the hour before opening, the cast is

- Raking the walks
- Washing the plants
- Checking the restaurant exhausts to calibrate and strengthen with the day's winds

- Setting the music and background noises
- Repairing every scratch and dent on the buildings
- Checking every costume
- Doing last-minute rehearsals of activities
- Checking all the props and repairing or replacing as needed
- Painting the grass. Seriously. Despite impeccable lawn care, once in a while a brown spot appears. Unacceptable. All brown spots are painted green every morning.

Disney's guests come for a day or a few days. Your new employee is becoming part of your cast. Isn't his or her day one experience even more important?

You are wondering how Disney treats its new cast members and partners.

One Disney group hired a new advertising agency. They invited the agency team to come to Disney World for an orientation. The president of the agency showed up late, missed the opening dinner, and checked into his Disney hotel by himself.

"Good evening."

"Checking in, please."

"Of course. Long day?"

"Yep. Missed my plane."

"I'm sorry. Did you have dinner?"

"No. Come to think of it, I didn't."

"Room service normally closes at 10:00. I'll call them to make sure they stay open for you."

"Thank you."

Ten minutes after the agency president got to his room, room service called him to see if he wanted anything. He did. It showed up fifteen minutes later. Five minutes after that, the person from the front desk called to make sure the agency president had everything he needed.

That agency president didn't need to see anyone paint the grass to understand Disney's fanatical approach to making people feel welcome.

Tool 10.2 can help you think through and plan your new employee's day one experience.

Tool 10.2

New Employee as Valued Customer (Downloadable)

Why new employee was offered the job:

- *Delilah has required strengths as achiever, discipline, focus (as well as responsibility and self-assurance)*
- *Delilah is a practiced water resource manager and physics expert*

Why new employee accepted the job:

- *Fits with Delilah's core values of doing good for others and valuing the environment*
- *Fits with Delilah's affinity for working in pairs in a sociable group with a hands-off manager*
- *Moves Delilah forward toward a future as director of product supply*

Overlapping points to leverage in welcome experience:

- *Doing good for others; working in pairs; sociability*

Pre-start letter/package night before start: *Hal to arrange*

Who greets the new employee: *Jill*

How to greet the new employee: *Pre-work coffee*

Where to greet the new employee: *At cafe*

Entrance signs and symbols: *No signs, but Jill to alert Anna and shift team to be at base as they arrive*

Welcome signs and symbols in their work area: *N.A.*

Points to make or avoid in introducing new employee to others: *Her water resource management experience*

Day-one activities: *Morning coffee; group lunch*

Day-one close out and take homes (for supporters at home): *Debrief with Anna; sampling of Goodfood's food to take home*

Start by reminding yourself why you choose this new employee and why you think he or she accepted the job. Use your insight to design the welcome experience. Think through these eight basic steps:

1. Pre-start letter/package. Because you helped your new employee get a head start, why not also get a head start on boosting his or her excitement? No need to be elaborate. A simple handwritten note delivered to your employee's house or hotel before the start can make a big difference. You can reduce first-day jitters by including information about what time to arrive, what to wear, where to park, where to go, scheduled appointments, what to bring, what not to bring, and so on.

2. Who will greet your new employee? Ideally, you. Though in some cases you may want a peer to be the first to say hello.

3. How will you greet your new employee? Think through whether you want to orchestrate a big entry or a subtle entry. Different approaches are better in different situations. Think it through and make a choice. Recirculate or reference your original announcement the day before your new employee starts so coworkers can refresh their memories.

4. Where will you greet your new employee? In the lobby? In a coffee shop or café down the street? Again, just have a plan.

5. Put welcome signs and symbols in your new employee's work area. A simple note? Flowers? A huge banner? The note could be from you, the team, the CEO. Welcome signs and symbols are easy to implement, and they make a big impact.

6. Script the points you will make about your new employee when you make introductions (also note the points you are going to avoid). Your goal is to make your new employee feel welcome, valuable, and valued. Avoid saying anything that will make anyone feel bad in any way.

7. Plan day-one activities. Everything communicates, especially at the start of any new venture. Your new employee will remember the time you spend with him on day one for a long time. And the time you didn't spend with him, particularly if he is left to his own devices to figure things out. Your day-one actions and inactions can undo all of your good work to date. Pay close attention to your agenda.

8. The way the day ends will be foremost in your new employee's mind when he goes home and his family asks the inevitable question, "How did it go?" Close the day on a high note. Think about sending your new employee home with a welcome package of the company's logo items for his or her supporters. You want your new employee to feel welcome, valuable, and valued. And you also want his or her supporters to believe they are welcome, valuable, and valued, so that they will reinforce those feelings.

We did something a little personal. First, assigned the workspace, got the equipment, and had a standardized company gift basket. The bottom is a company lunch pouch and the entire basket is filled with logo items, munchies, and things that make someone part of the team (pens, t-shirts, caps, coffee cups) that is on the new hire's desk when they arrive. They also have a lunch invite from a "PAL" a specially trained "professional assistance liaison" from a different department who takes them out the first week so they have a resource outside of their department. Other PALs spend an hour with the new hire in the first two days after the company and benefit orientation explaining how what they do fits into the company's delivery of service and aligns with the mission. They are also toured, the manager gets a checklist, and they are checked in by HR. Not expensive but highly personal and well received. When temps convert to full time the first thing they want is that gift basket. Just a fun touch.

—PrimeGenesis Client

PROTOTYPICAL DAY-ONE SCHEDULE

Pre-start: Morning coffee with direct supervisor (you).
Opening: Informal gathering with team for meet and greet.
AM: Onboarding conversations.
Lunch: With core team.
PM: Activities that reinforce message, onboarding conversations.
Close: Debrief with direct supervisor.

Pick the Right Day One

Start by picking the right day one. It doesn't have to be the day payroll starts. It does have to be a day when you and your new employee's most important colleagues will be in the office. The symbolism of your welcome speaks volumes about how you truly regard this new player, and your team will be inclined to follow your lead. So be welcoming, gracious, and very, very pleased to have your new employee onboard. If something comes up to keep you out of the office on day one, pick a new day one.

Broadcast Your Certainty about and Commitment to Your Onboarding Employee

Your relationship with your new employee is probably the most significant relationship in his or her work life. Most employee turnover is ultimately caused by problems with that relationship. Make it clear to your employee and everyone else from the very start that you will do everything in your power to inspire and enable this individual.

Matthew chose the more experienced hire, Jenny, over the rising star. The new position was tricky and Jenny was going to have to build alliances fast. While Matthew was confident in Jenny, her ability to build those alliances was going to be key to her success over time. Matthew waited to see how Jenny would do.

This story does not have a happy ending. Jenny did a good job building some alliances, but failed to identify all the stakeholders. Since Matthew had not reached out to those people by asking them to support Jenny, they didn't bother contacting her themselves. In the end, those people found other ways to get done what they needed to get done, and Jenny was shut out.

Once you make the offer and your new employee accepts, that individual becomes, unequivocally, absolutely your right hire. That's all there is to it. Pepper your day one plan with action items that illustrate your endorsement:

Message: Your new employee is personally important to you, and you care about his or her emotional engagement.

Action: Take your new employee to lunch—someplace nice. This little effort demonstrates a culture of inclusiveness. People aren't engaged, if they aren't included. And engagement drives results.

Message: I will do everything I can to inspire and enable you to succeed.

Action: Make sure your onboarding employee's work area is complete, comfortable, and that every detail has been attended to so that he or she can get down to real work right away.

HIRING MANAGER ALERT

If your new employee is not, in your heart of hearts, unequivocally, absolutely your right hire, stop; do not pass Go; rescind the offer. Or find some way to make the individual you chose absolutely the right hire for some modified role. A hiring manager's certainty and commitment is requisite to successful employee onboarding.

GUEST EXPERT

David Lee on the Emotional Side[2]

David Lee has written extensively about the emotional side of onboarding. He preaches the importance of making your new employees feel welcomed, comfortable, secure, proud, excited, inspired, and confident. After one conference, he wrote down some thoughts about onboarding that welcomes and inspires, based on what he'd heard from people at Ritz-Carlton, Southwest Airlines, and Texas Roadhouse.

1. Examine your orientation program and ask:
   - "What emotions does our orientation program likely elicit?"
   - "What emotions do we want to elicit?
   - How can we do that?"
2. In your employee orientation program, share more stories that communicate what makes your organization great—that is, stories that elicit pride.
3. Share more stories that show how employees make a difference, how they matter.
4. Perhaps you can make your own . . . videos. Include interviews with leaders and frontline employees, and share stories of the pride-worthy things your company is doing.

(continued)

(*continued*)

5. Take the best hotelier in your area out to lunch and ask them what they do to make their guests feel welcomed. Ask them what they pay attention to and how they create memorable guest experiences. Think of how you can adapt this to your orientation onboarding process.

6. And of course, ask your new employees for feedback on what you can do to create a more emotionally engaging onboarding experience.[3]

NOTE TO HR

Do your own documentation and appraisal of day one. Your central function and broker role put you in the perfect position to share successes across the organization.

You and your new employee are off and running, buoyed by good feelings, goodwill, optimism, and organizational support. That's a day one that makes positive and true first impressions both ways.

TIME-SAVER

Standard operating procedure is for new employees to spend day one filling out forms, settling into their workspace, and meeting people informally. What a missed opportunity!

Managing day one to make positive impressions both ways jump-starts relationships in a big way.

Two ideas:

1. Create a prototypical day-one agenda that you can adjust to fit each new employee's situation. Continually evaluate and evolve that prototypical agenda as you learn.

2. Set aside one day each month for group orientations. This will allow you to make the orientations a bigger deal with more regular senior management involvement. Monthly orientation also facilitates creation of onboarding cohorts.

Summary and Indicated Actions

Managing first impressions goes two ways: the impression the new employee makes on the organization and the impression the organization makes on the employee. None of this is underhanded or secret. Each should work to make the best possible first impression on the other. There are some basic ideas that always help.

First, in terms of the impression the new employee makes on the organization:

- Serve as a scout for new employees, letting them know what time to arrive, where to park, what to wear, what to bring, and so on.
- Help your new employees design day one experiences that seed their messages.

Next, in terms of the impression the organization makes on the new employee:

- Do a reality check on what's really going on inside the organization. You can't get the organization to pretend to be something that it's not. You can manage the new employee's expectations so they're not surprised.

- Design a superlative new employee experience for your new employees so they feel welcomed, valued by, and valuable to an organization they will take pride in.

  Finally, from both perspectives:

- Pick the right day one—a time and a place when and where you and your new employee's most important colleagues can be there to greet him or her and participate in the day-one activities.
- Don't reinvent the wheel. Start with our prototypical day-one plan, and modify it to fit your situation.

Focus

- *Manager:* Manage first impressions. Welcome. Introduce your new employee.
- *Employee:* Manage first impressions.
- *Human Relations:* Manage implementation of day-one plan.

CHAPTER 11

Speed Development of Important Working Relationships

Enable and Inspire

Total Onboarding Program (TOP)				
Align>	Acquire>	Accommodate>	Assimilate>	Accelerate>
			Day One IV. Enable and Inspire	
			Resources, support, follow-through. (12)	
			Speed important working relationships. (11)	
			Make positive first impressions both ways. (10)	
		III. Big Head Start		
	II. Recruit			
I. Prepare				

"Introduce" is a transitive action verb meaning, among other things, to cause to be acquainted. Just giving someone a list of people to meet and hoping something happens is not enough to cause that person to be acquainted with anyone.

Take the joining in/assimilation challenge off the table for your new employee. You didn't hire him or her for strengths in assimilating. You hired him or her for what he or she can do and get others to do. However, no one gets anything valuable done without productive working relationships with others. So do anything and everything you can to make your new employee's assimilation as easy as possible.

Assimilation is a big deal. Doing it well makes things far easier for everyone. Getting it wrong triggers relationship risks, which increase delivery risks. There are some basic steps that make a huge difference. We suggest you set up meaningful, productive onboarding conversations for your new employees with members of their formal and informal/shadow networks and tap into opportunities and events than can help them strengthen their networks. We also suggest that you do periodic check-ins with those networks. If issues arise, you want to know about them early so you can help your new employee adjust.

TIME-SAVER

Assimilation, or speeding up the development of important working relationships is a main step of onboarding and a core plank of getting new employees up to speed. So much so that many people define *onboarding* as assimilation coaching. While onboarding encompasses more than just assimilation, the ideas in this chapter are critical components of getting new employees up to speed in half the time.

Cirque du Soleil has refined its way of assimilating new artists while preserving their spark. As Lyn Heward describes in *The Spark*, "Our goal is to make the artists comfortable in just about every way possible, so we can make them uncomfortable in their thinking—challenge them, destabilize them. The more we do that, the more they will throw themselves into their roles."[1] This is exactly what you are trying to do with your new employee: make him or her comfortable enough with others to think freely.

Assimilation Is About Adjusting to the Culture[2]

Culture can be referred to as "the way we do things here." It's what people do and say, informed by their underlying core values. While people generally learn about culture starting with the most superficial (what people say about their culture), culture is rooted in what people really are. A good shorthand we learned from one of our clients is "Be. Do. Say." It works for both people and organizations:

- **Be:** The underpinning of culture (and integrity) is what people really are, their core values, assumptions, beliefs, and intentions.

- **Do:** These are behavioral, attitudinal, and communication norms that can be seen, felt, or heard such as signs and symbols like physical layouts, the way people dress, talk to each other, and interact with each other.

- **Say:** What people say about culture can be found in things like mission statements, creeds, and stories. As Edgar Schein points out, these articulate the professed culture.[3]

For a culture to be sustainable, *be, do, say* must be in sync. It is relatively easy to see when people's actions don't match their words. It is far more difficult to figure out when words and actions match but don't align with underlying assumptions and beliefs. Yet when that happens, those people's words and actions will change over time. Just as your own *be, do, say* needs to line up, the same is true for an organization's.

A strong culture can be a sustainable competitive advantage. Indeed, there are some who argue that it is the only sustainable competitive advantage. Plants can be built. Brands can be bought. People move on. But the culture remains.

It's hard for anyone to figure out a new culture alone. But your new employee isn't on his or her own. You're there to help. You are going to share what you know about the culture, going well beyond "the way things are done around here" to why they're done that way. You are going to help your new employee adjust to the new culture (culturalization) and help build mutually beneficial relationships with the most important stakeholders (socialization). This is what assimilation is all about

HURDLE

Figuring Out a New Culture

- **Problem:** It is difficult for a new employee to figure out a new culture on his or her own.

- **Solution:** Help your new employee figure out the culture by talking him or her through what you know about what people say, do, and believe.

Taking the time to culture train new talent eliminates a great deal of timidity and reduces the time required to develop the person's individual comfort level within the peer group. The basic exchange defines each individual's expertise, limitations, associations, and their hot buttons along with their best line of reproach. It must be a soul bearing exchange to the extent that it provides the new hire with clear insight to the personalities of the individuals on the team as well as the overall group culture.

—*PrimeGenesis Client*

Who You Know versus What You Know

Patty was clearly the smartest person in the room in almost any meeting. Combining that with her extensive experience in the finance function made her a complete powerhouse. She was self-confident and self-reliant and a real value to any organization to which she belonged.

When Patty joined a company as divisional CFO, she spent a fair amount of time over her first couple of months immersing herself in the numbers so that she could get up to speed quickly and build the knowledge required to make the contributions she knew she could make. She went to all the appropriate meetings, but sat in the back listening until she felt ready to add value; and her manager was fine with that.

Unfortunately, two months into her job, the company decided to merge Patty's division with another. The other division's CFO had been in place for a couple of years and was doing a good job and got the new combined job. The company tried to find another role for Patty somewhere else in the company, but few people knew her, fewer had worked closely with her, and no one was ready to stand up for her. She ended up leaving the company.

This is an extreme (but not unique) example of *who* you know (or don't know) being more important than *what* you know.

Who Serves Whom?

Contrast that story with Ted who joined a different company as head of product development. The business had traditionally been run at the regional level with each region having its own capability to create, manufacture, market, sell, and deliver regionally appropriate products. Ted's predecessor built a central product development group, but had failed to get any of the regional presidents to support its efforts.

Ted started by going out to visit with each regional president one-on-one. He sat down with each and said, "I know we run this business at the regional level. I see the role of the central product development group as supporting the regions. Given that, I'm here to start to understand what you need from us to help you and your team achieve its goals."

He then spent the next six months assembling and directing resources to help the regions.

Not surprisingly, the regional presidents were delighted to have their people spend time and share their issues and opportunities with Ted and his team. And when Ted and his team started delivering on their promises of support and innovative new products that helped the regional presidents and their teams build business, the regional presidents became fans.

Assimilation as a Predictor of Success

A study of IBM interns in 2004 by Chang et al. found that the success of those interns' assimilation into the group was directly correlated with their propensity to return full time to IBM after the internship. They found that awareness of the knowledge and skills of others, and accessibility of others were strong predictors of propensity to return.[4] (Read that as a proxy for onboarding success.)

- **Awareness:** How well the knowledge and skills of each person are understood
- **Information access:** Extent to which each person is accessible within a sufficient time frame with needed information or advice
- **Information seeking:** How often information or advice is sought on projects, work, or operations from other individuals
- **Social closeness:** How often each person is met with for non-work-related activities

The point is that it's not about the *quantity of interactions*. It's about the *quality of the relationships*. As the University of Virginia's Robert Cross makes clear, it's far better to build mutually valuable relationships with a relatively small set of central connectors and brokers, than to build acquaintances with a wide range of peripheral players.[5]

- **Central connectors:** Leaders, experts, old timers, gateway roles, or political players. Often bottlenecks and vulnerabilities. (Directly connecting with information or resources).

- **Brokers:** Leverage ability to drive change, diffusion, or innovate. These people can also fill liaison or cross-process roles (linking with others who have information or resources).

- **Peripheral players:** Less well-connected or less interested in helping with access to information or resources.

Cross's *brokers* may be the rising stars. They are the up-and-coming people driving things. They're relatively easy to spot and relatively open to helping. They are well worth connecting with. Steer your new employee toward *brokers*.

The world is full of *peripheral players* who want to connect. Many of them will be open to building social closeness. The trouble is that they have neither the knowledge or skills to help, nor strong enough relationships with others who do. They may be seductively distracting. Keep your new employee from wasting time with *peripheral players*.

Too many people ignore the *central connectors*—often because they've been in position for an extended period of time and are looked down on by people rising around them. Yet this is where a lot of institutional knowledge resides. As Rob Cross explains, "Central connectors have a lot of ties. 3–5 percent of people manage 20–25 percent of the information flows."[6]

Don't expect your new employee to be able to figure out who the people with valuable knowledge and skills are. Don't wait for him or her to discover the most valuable people. Point out key *brokers* and *central connectors*, and make the connections.

New Employees Need Your Help, Not Just Your Encouragement

There are many things you can do to help your new employee assimilate. We're going to take you through five that are particularly important. Don't leave assimilation to chance. You don't want to see if your new employee will sink or swim. That's not the test. The test is whether he or she can deliver the results you need with all the help you can provide. Start with a proactive approach in the five areas we delineate here and in Tool 11.1. Identify the most valuable people for your new employee to work with. Make those connections first:

1. Introduce your new employee to *stakeholders* for meaningful and productive onboarding conversations (up, across, down; internal, external; information providers, resource controllers; suppliers, customers; cross-hierarchy, cross-function, cross-region).

2. Introduce your new employee to *behind-the-scenes networks* like sports teams, communities of common interest, and so on.

3. Assign your new employee to special *projects* that can further assimilation.

4. Invite your new employee to *meetings and events* that can further his or her assimilation.

5. Introduce your new employee to connecting *tools* (organization directory, mentor, buddy, cohort, touchstone, blogs, wikis).

1. Stakeholders

Introduce your new employee to stakeholders for meaningful and productive onboarding conversations (up, across, down; internal, external; information providers, resource controllers; suppliers, customers; cross-hierarchy, cross-function, cross-region).

It's a little scary how often people tell us their company has a really good onboarding program which turns out to consist of an orientation followed by giving new employees a list of 20 to 30 people with whom they should set up onboarding conversations. Those two things are not bad. They are just woefully inadequate.

Introduce is a transitive action verb meaning, among other things, to cause to be acquainted. Just giving someone a list of people to meet and hoping something happens does not cause that person to be acquainted with anything. Setting up the meetings; providing brief bios, background, or useful information; and clarifying the specific objective of interactions with both parties should be your minimum standard when you introduce your new employee to stakeholders. Conversations need to be two-way. Each participant should walk away with a deeper understanding of the others' perspective and strengths so they will work together better.

Tool 11.1

Assimilation Checklist (Downloadable)

Introduction to stakeholders for onboarding conversations (up, across, down; internal, external; information providers, resource controllers; suppliers, customers; cross-hierarchy, cross-function, cross-region)

> Up: *Anna (head of product supply), Bart (organization president)*
>
> Across: *Jill (work partner), Charlie (head of water retrievers), Devon (head of operations center), Edgar (water retriever shift supervisor), Fran (operations center shift supervisor), Gina (main contact in operations center), and Hal (HR)*
>
> Down: *Ingrid, Jack Jr., Kia, Larry (water transporters)*
>
> External: *Mary from water co., Norb from Weather.com, Oscar from city*
>
> Info: *Peter*
>
> Resources: *Quentin*

Introduction to informal, behind-the-scenes networks like sports teams, communities of common interest, etc.

> *Softball team: Robert*
>
> *Hunting club: Sandra*

Invitation to events that can further new employee's assimilation

> *Orientation: First Friday*
>
> *Cross-divisional plans: Review in 4 weeks*
>
> *Cross-divisional recruiting practices: Examine again in 2 weeks*

Assignment to special projects that can further new employee's assimilation

> *New customer pitch: 8 weeks out*

Introduction to connecting tools (organization directory, mentor, buddy, cohort, touchstone, blogs, wikis)

> *Mentor: Tom*
>
> *Buddy: Fran*
>
> *Touchstone: Uhlma*
>
> *Connect with divisional blog*

SIGNS AND SYMBOLS TO CONSIDER ABOUT ONBOARDING CONVERSATIONS

Make the call to set up onboarding meetings with stakeholders yourself to signal how much you value the stakeholder and the conversation.

Prepare stakeholders for the onboarding meeting by providing bio or background info on the new employee along with the recruiting brief and/or your Total Onboarding Plan to signal how much you value the stakeholder and the conversation.

Prepare the new employee for the onboarding meetings by providing bio or background info on the stakeholders to signal how much you value the new employee, the stakeholder, and the conversation.

- **Message:** We're taking this new position seriously.
- **Action:** Prepare all players for the most productive onboarding conversations possible.

Ideally you and your new employee co-created a comprehensive stakeholder list as part of the new employee's personal onboarding plan (chapter 7). So we won't go into that here. Do take another look at the informal networks towards which you plan to steer your new employee because they're always evolving. Make sure to introduce your new employee to information providers and resource controllers—wherever they sit in the formal organization chart.

FOR NEW EMPLOYEE

Make sure your new employee takes these conversations seriously. The way he or she handles these conversations can make a big impact on what the stakeholders think of your new employee—and of you.

2. Behind-the-Scenes Networks

We can almost guarantee that you are part of at least one behind-the-scenes network. These don't show up on any organization chart anywhere. Yet, they often explain seemingly unexplainable information flows. Think about people exchanging information in car pools, bowling alleys, on trains, softball fields, golf courses, hunting trips, recruiting trips, at volunteer events, school events, church events. . . .

Almost every employee in almost every organization finds him- or herself in some situation outside of normal work hours with someone else from the organization. Inevitably they talk about their organization. These are the behind-the-scenes networks where relationships build over time.

Chip was a finance guy. Dave was a marketing guy in the same company. They fished together for years. As each of them moved up the ladder or into different roles, they helped each other connect to people who might be helpful. Eventually, Chip became CEO and Dave became chief marketing officer. The betting is that a lot of important decisions were really made on the banks of Chip and Dave's trout stream.

We're not saying behind-the-scenes networks are good or bad. They exist. The faster you can get your new employee tapped into some of them, the faster your new employee can start to build relationships and learn. Obviously, you won't be able to inject your new employee into all the behind-the-scenes networks. What you can and should do is connect your new employee with groups or individuals with common interests or hobbies. It's not hard for you to do, and it potentially has a huge impact.

REALITY CHECK

Don't force this one. Making a connection where there's an existing common interest is a good thing. Pushing people to accept a newcomer in an area where he or she does not naturally fit can be counterproductive.

A union environment has a culture like all others. There is the culture you can see and the culture that is working at the time clock, in break areas, the gate, or back office. . . .

. . . Unions often have their own induction efforts with employees. Yes, they talk about the contract, benefits, and employee rights, but it is now on a path to be different. As the Internet has grown in use, unions are communicating with their members at home on a wide

array of issues. Unions are devoting considerable funds on social networking infrastructure to better communicate with their members and their member's families.

—PrimeGenesis Client

HOT TIP

Make introductions to *key* people in the formal and informal networks (instead of all people).

Identifying *central connectors* and *brokers* then connecting your new employee with them is one of the most important ways to get your new employee up to speed in half the time. Don't let your employee waste time with friendly *peripherals* when you know who really controls information and resources.

NOTE TO HR

You may have more insight into informal networks than the hiring manager. Weigh in. It's not important for the hiring manager to look knowledgeable about this. It is important for the new employee to make the most valuable early connections. The same is true for behind-the-scenes networks.

Not all new employees, especially individual contributors, interview with HR. The recruiter has established the relationship and therefore the new employee thinks the recruiter is HR support. Human resources partners should introduce themselves to new employees in person, by phone, or by e-mail during the onboarding process. There should be a follow-up in 30 days to ensure each employee is settling in, the job is as described, and the manager has set goals and expectations.

3. Projects

Assigning your new employee to cross-functional projects is a great way for him or her to build a cross-functional network. Looking for special projects that offer opportunities for your new employee to work with people he or she normally would not work with is particularly important in early assignments as it is a way to preempt silo behavior.

Diana was named country president for her firm. Her boss assembled a team of people to spend a week with her in her new country to help her think things through. One of the people her boss picked was Jessie, who was relatively new to the region. This was a great opportunity for Jessie to get exposed to some other people from across the region and learn while contributing.

> *I have always required any new hires in support functions to work in the line of business or field for at least a week prior to filling the support job they were hired for.*
>
> —*PrimeGenesis Client*

NOTE TO HR

Identifying cross-functional, cross-divisional, cross-geographical projects that can help new employees connect with key players is another way you can help with assimilation. Since you are a *broker* yourself, you may have a broader perspective than hiring managers.

4. Meetings and Events

Meetings and events are great opportunities for new employees to work with and get to know broader groups of people. Have a bias to invite your new employee to as many meetings and events as possible.

One potentially important event is new employee orientation. Maude Divittis (probably Maude Divittis, PhD, by the time you read this) took us to task on this one. Her own practical learning and her research indicate that orientations can be particularly powerful, if done well. Here's her perspective.

Maude Divittis on Orientations[7]

Maude is a big believer in orientations—as one part of a complete onboarding strategy for individual leaders and their teams. As she puts it, "Much time, money, energy, and effort have been expended to identify, recruit, and hire a new executive. Although skills, experience, and relationships may give a candidate access to an exciting leadership opportunity, the success of a new executive relies on his or her ability to perform within a new context."

Orientations can be one critical element of an approach that "provides a filter and bridge between the new executive and the organization to ensure appropriate understanding of the organizational culture and norms, and the key roles and actions to accelerate individual and team performance." In particular, a strong orientation program can set new executives up to make informed decisions and build key relationships that are ongoing and sustainable.[8]

If you really want to make an impact, think preparation—delivery—follow-through. If there's someone in a meeting you want your new employee to become acquainted with, let both people know about your objective in advance. Make the introduction during the meeting. Then, make sure your new employee follows through to build on the new acquaintance after the meeting.

5. Tools

This is one of those sections that will most definitely be out of date by the time you read it. So don't follow our detailed prescription here; follow the principle. The principle is that you should identify and use all of the most important tools at your disposal to help your new employee assimilate into your organization. Let's touch on a couple as examples:

- **Organizational directory:** Most schools have them. They're really useful for matching names and faces. Today, they're mostly electronic, relatively easy to put up, and generally well worth the investment—particularly for assimilating new employees.
- **Mentor:** Assigning a relatively senior person to help your new employee learn the lay of the land generally has a big impact.

- **Buddy:** This is different from a mentor in that it's someone at the same level as your new employee who can answer trivial questions without fear of repercussions. Another winning idea.

- **Cohort:** If you are bringing in several people at the same time, you can turn them into a cohort by routing them through the same orientation program and even formally facilitating follow-up cohort meetings so they can share their experiences. Cohort orientation gives participants another set of buddies to talk to.

- **Touchstone:** This one's for more senior people. The idea is to give senior employees a buddy who is at least three levels below them in the organization. This person can tell the senior leader what's really going on and how his or her messages are really being received.

- **Blogs and wikis:** Make sure you tap your new employee into the most important blogs, wikis, and new information-sharing tools, both internally and externally so he or she can start to listen to the chatter and participate in discussions.

NOTE TO HR

You've got three tasks here:

1. Let the new employee know about available tools.
2. Let the hiring manager know about available tools.
3. Create new tools to facilitate even better social networking going forward.

GUEST EXPERT

Rob Cross on Social Networks

Rob Cross of the University of Virginia has been studying social networks for a decade. He and his Network Roundtable have discovered that high performers have *noninsular* networks. They reach out up, across, and down in a number of important ways:

Up: They reach up in the hierarchy to understand the strategic context, secure resources and political support.

Across: They reach across to get insight from different divisions and brainstorm with those who face similar challenges.

Partners: They reach out to external experts and partners for innovative ideas and novel opportunities.

Clients: They reach out to clients internally and externally for input on how to keep their work on target to add value.[9]

Rob and his colleagues identified five myths for new hires and some ways for hiring managers to combat these:

Myth 1: The best newcomers can fend for themselves. (Not true)

So, savvy managers "continually encourage new hires to ask questions while also reminding others to expect and respond to such requests on a timely basis."

Myth 2: A massive information dump allows newcomers to obtain what they need. (Necessary but not sufficient)

So, managers should:

— "Emphasize relationship development as a means of facilitating information transfer."

— Emphasize explanations of organizational roles and responsibilities.

— Refer newcomers to in-house experts and other key resources, contacting those people in advance so newcomers won't be cold calling.

— Examine newcomers' ever-evolving list of relationships to spot and fill gaps.

— Allow time for socializing.

— Invite newcomers to key meetings so they can learn about group dynamics, personalities, power structures, and decision-making norms.

Myth 3: Cursory introductions are all that's needed (Not nearly good enough).

Key is to make sure the new hire and the people he or she meets understand each other's roles and responsibilities so they can connect as appropriate later. The newcomer's manager should leverage meetings, lunches, and company gatherings to facilitate face-to-face meetings.

(continued)

(*continued*)

Myth 4: First assignments should be small, compact, and quickly achievable (Wrong).

Key is to give new employees initial assignments that require them to build relationships with a wide variety of people. So, managers should:

— Design the first project so that it can't be completed without assistance from coworkers.

— Assign newcomers to cross-functional project teams that expose them to a broad network of resources.

— Give new hires the opportunity to develop a unique expertise that others must access to complete their own work.

— Review progress on the first assignment by asking not only, "What have you accomplished?" but also "Whom have you talked to?"

Myth 5: Mentors are best for getting newcomers integrated. (Mentors are good; but buddies are even better for answering trivial or politically sensitive questions.)

So, managers should make sure new hires have at least one other coworker who serves as a buddy.[10]

All in all, Rob is convinced that relational onboarding is dramatically more important than informational onboarding. As he puts it:

> Too often companies just throw information at people and don't invest in creating relationships. Awareness of knowledge is a strong predictor of success. . . . It's not just about mapping information, but setting up conditions for use.
>
> We think what's required is smart mentoring to connect newcomers with brokers through structured introductions. It literally triples the connectivity of a newcomer. Think about this not only in terms of newcomers reaching out to people, but people reaching out to them. It legitimizes them. It reduces departures—particularly for experienced hires moving into a strong culture.
>
> The companies that took onboarding more seriously made introductions not just "nice to haves" but mandatory and taken seriously. They found ways to profile newcomers' expertise so they were drawn into discussions with others. The first assignment should require connecting with others in the organization. That helps them get embedded—particularly in the zero to six-month time frame.[11]

Cherish the Differences

The good news is that if you do the things suggested in this chapter so far, you will be doing a far better job helping your new employee assimilate than most managers do. You will be miles ahead of the managers who just give their new employees a list of 20 to 30 people to talk to and leave them to it.

The bad news is that every new employee is different. Every new employee has his or her own history, perspective, needs, and desires. You are going to need to modify your approach to onboarding at least slightly for each new employee. Fortunately, there are some ways to group employees so that you can know what to expect. Look at their socioeconomic background. Look at their cultural background. Look at their work history. Obviously, your expectations of someone moving into his or her first job are going to be different from your expectations of a new senior employee.

Be alert to differences between generational cohorts. While we're not in any way suggesting anything resembling discrimination by age, we are suggesting that people born in different generations are going to have different perspectives and needs. Being aware of those differences will make you a more effective manager of all of your employees.

GUEST EXPERT

Tamara Erickson on Generations[12]

Tamara Erickson of the Concours Institute talks about differences in onboarding across four generational cohorts: Traditionalists (born 1928–1945), Baby Boomers (1946–1960), Generation X (1961–1980), and Generation Y (1981–2000).

TRADITIONALISTS (1928–1945)

Expect people of this generation to have a practical outlook and dedicated work ethic. They will tend to be respectful of authority and bow to leadership by hierarchy. They are prepared to make personal sacrifices in relationships and will be loyal to the organization. They believe hard work is good in itself. They were greatly influenced by the transportation and telecom age and deal with change

(continued)

(continued)

by getting it over with. They want a fair wage, stable employment, and a secure retirement. They were teens during World War II, saw the great economic boom, and got onboard the American Dream. They are rule makers and conformists.

Onboard these people by showing them respect, accommodating their needs, clarifying their roles, responsibilities, performance standards, and decision-making processes.

BABY BOOMERS (1946–1960)

Expect Boomers to have an optimistic outlook and a driven work ethic. They generally have a love/hate view of authority and believe in leadership by consensus. They seek personal gratification in relationships. Their loyalty is to their own career, and they work to meet or surpass their own expectations. They are competitive. They grew up during the information age. When it comes to change, they want to be the ones creating it. They want competitive wages, stable employment in meaningful work, and a comfortable and interesting retirement. Boomers were teens in the 1960s and 1970s, a time of causes and revolution, so they take charge of the change.

Onboard these people by putting them in charge, using give-and-take problem solving and decision making, encouraging them to compete, and giving them challenging work.

GENERATION XERS (1961–1980)

Expect Xers to have a skeptical outlook and a balanced work ethic. They are unimpressed by authority, instead believing in leadership by competence. They are reluctant to commit in relationships and have selective loyalty. They view work as a form of self-fulfillment. They grew up in the technology age and want to make change work for them. They want wealth, work-life balance, and early retirement. They were teens in the 1980s and 90s and saw disruption, social change. They thrive on rule morphing.

When onboarding Xers, keep in mind their general desire for work-life balance and ready access to interesting and meaningful work choices and development opportunities.

GENERATION YERS (1981–2000)

Look for people born at the end of the twentieth century to have a hopeful outlook and determined work ethic. As children of Baby Boomers, they have a polite view of authority and believe in leadership by pulling together. They tend to be inclusive in relationships and practice a balanced loyalty. They seek work as an opportunity for continuous learning and change. Growing up in a technology integration age they see change as inevitable, pervasive, and accelerating. They seek wealth accumulation and indulge in interests and curiosities. They were greatly influenced by a world filled with random terrorism and upheaval.

Onboard Yers with fast decision making, stimulating work, continuous feedback, frequent praise, working in teams, support networks, and continuous learning and change.

Here's a checklist of approaches for involving parents in your recruiting activities of Yers:

- Distribute packs of information for parents to students at universities and job fairs.
- Hold a career fair in your community designed specifically for parents.
- Create special FAQ material directed at parents' likely questions and concerns (retirement, health benefits, 401(k) plans, educational opportunities, and so on).
- Hold parent orientation sessions or conference calls.
- Invite parents of interns and new hires to visit the Yer's place of work and meet the boss and colleagues.
- Provide the staffing necessary to follow through with parent requests.
- Run ads communicating your positive attributes as an employer aimed at parents.
- Provide incentives for parents to refer their children (beginning with your current employees—if your current employees won't refer their own children, consider whether you really are a good employer).
- Include parents in employee benefits.

Cross-Border Assimilation

There are many books on this subject so we won't go into a great deal of depth here. The main point is that people will forgive almost any cross-border assimilation mistakes except arrogance. Whether you are bringing your new employees into a new country, region, industry, or organization with its own culture, make sure they know that it is their responsibility to assimilate into the culture and not the organization's responsibility to adapt to them.

During Jean's first year in Japan, he never sat down in a meeting until someone told him where to sit. In some meetings, he was the most important person in the room and sat in the seat of honor. In other meetings, he was less important. No one minded his asking. They took it as a sign of respect for the cultural differences and a willingness to be coached. On the other hand, people would have been upset and uncomfortable if he'd sat in the wrong place based on the arrogant view that he knew what was right.

You shouldn't worry too much about your new employees sitting in the wrong place, saying the wrong thing, or doing the wrong thing. That's going to happen. You should help them adjust their mindset so they seek to understand the new culture instead of merely applying their old way of being, doing, saying to the new situation.

Technology Can Help

At one level, telephones and videoconferences enable interactions across geographies. Some of the social mapping tools can give new employees insight into the social networks even before they start. As we saw in chapter 9, many organizations use electronic onboarding systems and portals to facilitate accommodation.

When it comes to assimilation, some technology can supplement face-to-face interactions. Sun Microsystems uses an onboarding game that guides new employees through various stages of learning and interaction with others. A big part of this is learning and accommodation; but it also provides assimilation opportunities through the interactions.

The point on technology (at least at the time this is being written) is to use it to help with assimilation, not lead it. The lead technology needs to be face-to-face interaction.

Periodic Check-Ins

Adjusting is a big part of a new employee's onboarding. As they assimilate into the new culture, they are going to have some missteps. That's okay. Some people will become early supporters of the new employee. Some people will be put off by the new employee. That's par for the course.

It's extremely helpful if you or your HR partner can do some sort of periodic check-in along the way. It doesn't have to be all that formal. It just has to give you some sort of read on what the new employee is doing and saying that's working well and what things he or she could do even better.

The premise here is that the earlier and more frequently you can reinforce the things that are working well and help correct the things that are working less well, the easier the new employee's assimilation will be.

MASTER CLASS

Create a newcomers' club with executive sponsors. A newcomers' club helps new employees learn from each other's and executive sponsors' experiences and connections. It gives executives opportunities to get informal feedback from people with fresh eyes, signal the importance of onboarding, reinforce their vision and values, and deliberately practice helping people at all levels assimilate into the organization.

Summary and Indicated Actions

We suggest you take a proactive approach to assimilating your new employee into the broader group with a particular focus on the most important relationships by:

1. Introducing your new employee to *key stakeholders* for onboarding conversations (up, across, down; internal, external; information providers, resource controllers; suppliers, customers; cross-hierarchy, cross-function, cross-region).

2. Introducing your new employee to *behind-the-scenes networks* like sports teams, communities of common interest, and so on.

3. Assigning your new employee to *special projects* that can further his or her assimilation.

4. Inviting your new employee to *meetings and events* that can further his or her assimilation (including, but not limited to orientations).

5. Introducing your new employee to *connecting tools* (directory, mentor, buddy, cohort, touchstone, blogs, wikis).

That's the generally applicable piece. At the same time, take into account the socioeconomic, experience, cultural, and generational differences in your new employees. Show *Traditionalists* respect, while giving them clarity. Put *Boomers* in charge and challenge them. Give *Xers* interesting and meaningful work choices and opportunities. Stimulate *Yers* with fast decisions, and continuous, frequent feedback and praise. And mind the cultural differences.

Focus

- **Manager:** Facilitate new employee assimilation initiatives. Be alert to challenges.

- **Employee:** Must invest in assimilating into the formal and informal networks.

- **Human Resources:** Support. Coach new employee and manager. Provide required resources.

CHAPTER 12

Provide Resources, Support, and Follow-Through

Enable and inspire

Total Onboarding Program (TOP)				
Align>	Acquire>	Accommodate>	Assimilate>	Accelerate>
			Day One IV. Enable and Inspire	
			Resources, support, follow-through. (12)	
			Speed important working relationships. (11)	
			Make positive first impressions both ways. (10)	
		III. Big Head Start		
	II. Recruit			
I. Prepare				

Make sure your new employee puts in place the building blocks of a high-performing team, as appropriate to his or her position.

The first step in giving your new employees the resources and support they need is confirming your own requirement and appetite for change. If you only need your new employees to assimilate into the existing culture, you can probably mentor them yourself or with an internal coach. However, if achieving the desired results requires your new employees to assimilate into *and* transform the team at the same time, they will need external assistance. (If insiders could transform your culture, they would have done so already.)

TIME-SAVER

We thought about calling this chapter "acceleration." It's the last of the four main steps of onboarding and all about helping your new employee and his or her team deliver better results faster. The main point is that onboarding doesn't end with day one or even the early days. Providing your new employee with resources and support pays dividends for a long time.

Dara was hired to head up shipping for the new company created by the merger of a large company and smaller company. Senior management especially appreciated her big company background.

She had thought about doing a New Manager Assimilation (Tool 12.1) session on her first day. But the head of shipping at the smaller company merging into the new company didn't think that was a good idea. "That's not the way we do things at our small company. It reeks of big company processes. Why not just have one-on-one sessions with everybody and get to know them individually?"

As we helped Dara think through this situation we recognized a dilemma. If we forced the New Manager Assimilation process on the small company's head of shipping, he would feel that Dara didn't value his perspective. If we did things exactly the way the small company normally did things, nothing would change. So we modified the opening day breakfast session to give Dara a chance to answer the group's questions, kicking off assimilation and transformation at the same time.

With appropriate resources in place, make sure your new employee puts the building blocks of a high-performing team in place as appropriate.[1] Those five building blocks are:

1. Reaching clarity around what needs to be accomplished first (the imperative)

2. Reaching clarity around who's doing what by when along the way (milestones)

3. Selecting one or two accomplishments to deliver faster than normal (early wins)

Tool 12.1

New Manager Assimilation (Downloadable)

The Ulrich/GE new manager assimilation process gets questions on the table and resolved immediately that would fester without it. This is a useful session to conduct for a new manager.

STEP 1: Provide a brief introduction and an overview of the objectives of the session and review the process with all involved (team and new manager).

STEP 2: Team members, without the new leader present generate *questions* about:

i) Things about the new manager (professional, personal, including hopes, dreams, rumors, preconceptions, anything).

ii) The new manager as a team leader (what the manager knows about the team, priorities, work style, norms, communication, rumors).

iii) The new manager as a member of the broader organization (what the manager knows about the organization, how they fit, priorities, assumptions, expectations, rumors).

Plus the team should generate *ideas* for the new manager in the following areas:

i) What does the new manager need to know to be successful in new role?

What are the top three issues?

What are the secrets to being effective?

Are there any ideas for the new manager?

ii) What significant issues need to be addressed immediately?

Are there any quick fixes that are needed now?

Are there any difficult areas of the business that the new manager should know about?

iii) Other questions and ideas?

What is the one question that you are afraid to ask?

What additional messages do you have?

STEP 3: New manager rejoins teams to answer questions, listen, and learn.

---

4. Getting the right people in the right roles with the right support (roles)
5. Making sure everyone understands what everyone else is doing (communication)

Your new employee should get these building blocks in place on schedule (see Tool 12.2 for an example):

- *Imperative* in place in his or her first 30 days
- *Milestones* process in place by day 45
- *Early wins* identified by day 60 and delivered by month six
- *Roles* sorted by day 70, if appropriate
- *Communication* plan implemented on an ongoing basis

Tool 12.2
Acceleration Checklist (Downloadable)

Imperative
Resources available for new employee to get imperative in place by day 30
-Anna and Hal to help

Milestones
Resources available for new employee to get milestone management process in place by day 45
-Hal to share current template

Early Wins
Help employee select early win by day 60
-Hal to help

Role Sort
Encourage employee to think through role sort by day 70
-Hal to help

Communication
Resources available to support employee's communication plan
-Jill

Building Blocks of a High-Performing Team

On top of all the other demands you, your organization, and the realities of the situation make, your new employee must make implementing the building blocks of a high-performing team top priority. Your role is to EASE the way, *encouraging* progress, *aligning* efforts with those of others, *solving problems* the employee can't solve alone, and *ending distractions* that impede success.

Embed a *Burning Imperative* by Day 30

The starting point, and indeed the foundation for building a high-performing team is the *burning imperative* with its components of headline, mission, vision, objectives, goals, strategies, and values. Experienced, successful leaders inevitably say that getting people aligned around a vision and values is the most important thing they do. So if your new employee is in a leadership position, he or she needs to get others aligned around a burning imperative. If he or she is not directly leading others, your new employee and those with whom he or she works should align around *your* burning imperative.

    The burning imperative is a sharply defined, intensely shared, and purposefully urgent understanding from each of the team members of what they are "supposed to do, *now*," and how this works with the larger aspirations of the team and the organization. While mission, vision, and values are components of the burning imperative, the critical communication is the rallying cry that every one understands and can act on. Encourage your new employee to create and get buy in for a burning imperative in the first 30 days—even if it's only 90 percent right. Your new employee and his or her team will adjust and improve along the way.

BURNING IMPERATIVE

A clear, sharply defined, intensely shared, and purposefully urgent understanding of what the team is "supposed to do, *now*" and how this works with the larger aspirations of the team and the organization.

The burning imperative needs a shorthand summary or headline—most likely containing a strong, action-oriented verb. A brief statement or tagline reminds each team member of the entire range of work—from mission through strategy and the statements behind each step—and specifically of their commitments and responsibilities in relation to that work. For example, "Embed a strong burning imperative by day 30."

A burning imperative is *different* from a shared purpose. The difference is in the timing. Shared purpose drives the long term while your burning imperative drives the next phase of activity on the way to the long term. Remember the Apollo 13 example of "get these men home alive" after the accident in space. Clear. Sharply defined. Intensely shared. Purposefully urgent. It trumps all petty concerns. It didn't replace the overall shared purpose of exploring the universe to increase man's knowledge. The burning imperative moves the team forward on the way to that longer-term shared purpose.

Exploit *Milestones* to Drive Team Performance by Day 45

The real test of a high-performing team's capacity lies in the formal and informal practices that are at work across team members, particularly practices around clarifying decision rights and information flows. The real job of the team's leader is to inspire and enable others to do their absolute best, together. One way high-performing team leaders succeed is by integrating work across functions (as opposed to managing down). The milestone tool facilitates team integration by mapping and tracking what is getting done when by whom.

On one level, milestones are extraordinarily simple: who is doing what by when. On another level, the power unleashed by deploying a mutually supportive team-based follow-up system that helps everyone improve his or her performance versus goals is meaningful. Organizations that use this process in team meetings see dramatic improvements in team performance. Make sure your new employee adheres to these team meeting milestone management steps:

1. Before each meeting compile and circulate individual milestone updates to the team to take update sharing and reporting off the agenda, while maintaining a disciplined process to make sure information flows across the team.

2. In the first half of each meeting have each team member headline milestones wins, learning, and areas in which they need help from other team members. *Do not* work through anything at this point. Working items here reinforces a first-come, first-served mentality and causes people who share later in the order to get squeezed for time.

3. Pause at the halfway point of the meeting to prioritize milestones for discussion so that the team can use the balance of the meeting to discuss items in the right priority order instead of first come, first served. Priority is the team leader's judgment call. He or she will probably leave some items to be worked at a different time by a different group.

4. Use the second half of the meeting to discuss the overall team's most important issues and opportunities—milestone delivery in priority order. The team won't get through everything. That's okay because they are working the most important items first. This is the time to adjust as a team to make the most important goals.

5. Defer other items to the next meeting or a separate meeting.

If you attend too many of your employee's milestone meetings with his or her team, you will disempower your new employee. However, you can, and most certainly should, expect regular updates on milestones.

MILESTONES SHOULD CASCADE

Your new employee's team's milestones should be a subset of your milestones. Milestone management is a powerful way to keep everyone aligned, informed, on track, and progressing together.

Overinvest in *Early Wins* to Build Team Confidence by Day 60

Early wins are all about credibility and confidence. People have more faith in people who deliver. You want to have confidence in your new employee. You want team members to have confidence in your new employee, themselves, and the plan for change that has emerged with this new employee's contribution. Early wins fuel that confidence. So get your new employee and his or her team to identify potential early wins by day 60 and over invest to deliver by the end of the first six months—as a team.

Our early wins prescription is relatively simple. Your new employee should:

1. Select one or two early wins from the milestones list that
   - Will make a meaningful, external impact.
   - You (the boss) will want to talk about.
   - The team is sure it can deliver.
   - Model important behaviors.
   - Would not have happened if the new employee had not been in your employ.
2. Establish early wins by day 60, and deliver them by month six on the job.
   - Early means early. Select the wins early; communicate them early; and deliver them early.
   - Make sure the team understands the early wins and has bought into delivering them.
   - Early wins are the concrete results you need when someone asks how your new employee is doing.
3. Overinvest resources toward early wins to overdeliver.
   - Make sure your new employee does not skimp on early wins. He or she will need to invest more resources than expected to make sure the team delivers better and faster than anyone thought possible.
4. Stay alert and adjust quickly.
   - Your new employee must be closely involved in the progress of early wins and react immediately if anything starts to fall even slightly off track or behind schedule.
5. Celebrate and communicate early wins.
   - When your employee achieves his or her first early wins, celebrate the accomplishment with the entire team to reinforce the successful behavior.
   - Make sure your new employee communicates early wins in coordination with his or her ongoing communication plan.

In general, *early wins* are not synonymous with *big wins*. They are the early, sometimes small, yet meaningful wins that create momentum. They are the blasting caps, not the dynamite itself; the opening singles, not the grand-slam home run; the first successful test market, not the global expansion. They are generally found by accelerating something that's already in progress, not by starting something new. Early wins will generate credibility, confidence, momentum, and excitement.

OVERINVEST IN EARLY WINS

Because it is in your best interest for your new employee to succeed, it is in your best interest to over invest in early wins. Within the EASE framework, give more support than he or she requests. The payback is huge.

Secure ADEPT People in the Right *Roles* with the Right Support by Day 70

You and your new employee should strive to make your organization ever more ADEPT by acquiring, developing, encouraging, planning, and transitioning talent:

Acquire	Scope roles.
	Identify prospects.
	Recruit and select the right people for the right roles.
	Attract those people.
	Onboard them so they can deliver better results faster.
Develop	Assess performance drivers.
	Develop skills and knowledge for current and future roles.
Encourage	Provide clear direction, objectives, measures, and so on.
	Support with the resources and time required for success.
	Reinforce desired behaviors with recognition and rewards.
Plan	Monitor peoples' performance over time.
	Assess situation and potential.
	Plan career moves/succession planning over time.
Transition	Migrate people to different roles to fit their needs/life stage and company needs.

If you are reading this book, you probably already believe this is one of the most important things leaders do. Indeed, this book is all about the *acquire* piece of ADEPT. If your new employee is in a leadership position, help him or her jump-start ADEPT by getting the right people in the right roles with the right support to build a high-performing team.

MOVE FASTER ON THE TEAM

Push your new employees to move faster on people than they think they should. The risks of moving too fast are nothing compared to the damage that results when we leave people in the wrong place too long.

Drive Action with an Ongoing *Communication* Campaign

Everything communicates. Your new employee can either make choices about what to communicate in advance (as an act of leadership) or communicate in reaction to people and events. In our experience, the strongest leaders always take the communication offensive.

Ask your new employee to craft a communication plan that articulates his or her platform for change, vision, and call to action in a rallying message before trying to inspire anyone. Set your expectation that the communication plan will evolve with learning.

Guide your new employee to:

1. Identify and Understand the *Target Audiences*
   - What are your communication targets/audiences?
   - What is each audience currently thinking and doing with regard to your role in the organization?
   - What do you want each audience to stop doing, keep doing, or change?
   - What does each audience need to know to move from the current state to the desired state?
2. Craft the Message
   - Why do we need to change, in the context of your burning imperative? (Platform for change.)

- What will things look like after the change? (Vision. Help your new employee align all target audiences around one vision.)
- What should your audiences do next to move towards your vision? (Call to action.)
- Articulate a message that contemplates the platform for change, vision and call to action. The message should work for all target audiences. Keep it simple and transferable—like a bumper sticker message.

3. Plan the Campaign
   - How, when and with whom will you seed your message?
   - How and when will you launch your campaign?
   - How and when will you cascade your message?
   - How and when will you celebrate your early wins in the context of your message?
   - What else will you reinforce with your communication campaign?
   - Can you institutionalize your message? How?

4. Implement the Campaign

5. Monitor and Adjust
   - How will you measure success? When?
   - What are your contingency plans?

Push for a thoughtful message and a detailed campaign plan that you can track—in the same way you will track your new employee's milestones.

Get Feedback

Be diligent about gathering regular feedback on how your new employee's onboarding is progressing. Positive feedback creates opportunities to reinforce engagement. Negative feedback gives you a heads up on needed course corrections. Gathering feedback on your new employee is simple. Just ask your stakeholders and team members if they have any suggestions for you or your new employee to improve this onboarding.

Onboarding is also the perfect time for organizations to acquire feedback from new employees that can help them see the organization with fresh eyes. We recommend asking your onboarding employee one question at predefined checkpoints (week one, month one, month two, 100 days), for instance: "How likely is it that you would recommend [Company X] to a friend or colleague?"[2] Consider asking HR to create an anonymous feedback mechanism to gather responses. This is a great baseline question to pose to all employees once or twice a year.

To build organizational onboarding expertise and continuously improve new employee satisfaction, HR should review the Onboarding Track Record (Tool 2.2) with the newly onboarded employee at the end of month six. Human Resources is uniquely positioned to gather both hiring manager and employee perspectives. Divergent perspectives, if they emerge, will trigger suggestions about how to improve the onboarding process in your organization.

MASTER CLASS

Create a stable of internal and external mentors, coaches, and transition accelerators ready to help accelerate groups. To build expertise and institutionalize knowledge, have periodic meetings of the people in your stable to share learning about accelerating transitions in your organization.

Summary and Indicated Actions

By following the steps of a Total Onboarding Program, you increased the likelihood that you acquired, accommodated, and assimilated the right new employee in the right position. You and your colleagues have invested significant time and resources to get to this point. Don't even think about leaving your new employee to sink or swim from here on. This isn't a test. This isn't a game. It is a progression towards better results faster. Give your new employee the resources and support he or she needs to accelerate success.

1. Get your new employee the right support:

Situation	Need
Stable, time to learn	*Mentor* for knowledge sharing
Mixed, balance of learning and action	*Coach* for personal development
Hot landing, acute need to act fast	*Transition accelerator* to help jump-start team performance

2. Once support resources are in place, make sure your new employee establishes the building blocks of a high-performing team:

   • *Imperative* in place by day 30.

   • *Milestone* process in place by day 45.

   • *Early win* identified by day 60 and delivered by month six.

   • *Roles* sorted by day 70, if appropriate.

   • *Communication* plan implemented on an ongoing basis.

Focus

• *Manager:* Support. Mentor. EASE (Encourage—Align—Solve—End).

• *Employee:* Build the team. Deliver results.

• *Human Resources:* Support. Coach new employee and manager. Provide required resources.

Follow-Through

Done! You prepared for your new employee's success even before starting to recruit. You recruited in a way that reinforced messages. You helped your new employee get a head start. You enabled and inspired him or her to deliver better results faster. It's smooth sailing from here on.

In your dreams.

Sometimes it just doesn't work.

PrimeGenesis is as good as it gets at onboarding and transition acceleration. Since 2002, we've reduced the rate of new leader failure from 40 percent to 10 percent. There's good news and bad news here.

The good news is the fourfold reduction in failures. The bad news is that, even with our expert help, 10 percent of new leaders still fail. You will have onboarding failures.

The main sign that things are not working is a failure to deliver the required results. Often there are other signs along the way. Look for:

- *Role failure:* Often due to unclear or misaligned expectations and resources. Look for this if you see turf battles over responsibilities and resources.
- *Relationship failures:* Often due to early missteps. Look for this if you notice others' reluctance to work with your new employee or actively pushing against him or her.
- *Engagement failure:* Often due to the way you and your new employee work together. Look for this if your new employee starts avoiding conversation or extra efforts.
- *Personal failure:* Due to lack of strengths, motivation, or fit. This may be an underlying root cause of other failures.

The number-one thing that experienced, successful leaders regret is not moving faster on people when they discover problems. They regret settling for less than optimal performance from individuals or the team for too long. Moving people out of the wrong roles communicates volumes to the rest of the organization—as does not moving them, or moving too slowly. The hardest choices involve a strong individual performer who's damaging the team. Moving or not moving on a strong performer sends the loudest message of all about the relative importance of individuals and the team as a whole. You *must* protect the team.

We were working with one new leader and had the following conversation with her boss:

"How do you think Simone is doing?"

"She cannot do the job you put her in."

"I agree. Should I fire her now or wait until she's been here six months?"

"Why would you fire her? She's a terrific, talented person, and you invested a lot of time and effort to recruit. Why not find her a job she can do?"

The leader did. We bumped into Simone 12 months later in her new job at the same firm. She was confident, upbeat, making significant contributions to the organization, and clearly enjoying what she was doing.

The point is that getting new employees up to speed in half the time is going to reduce the risk of failure, not eliminate it. When you know it's not going to work, stop and redeploy. Maybe you can find a different role for that new employee that's better suited to his or her strengths and motivation. Under no circumstances, should you let an employee continue doing a job that won't work out. It's bad for them. It's bad for the team. It's bad for you.

Enabling and Inspiring Is an Ongoing Effort

As soon as someone stops learning and growing, he or she starts decaying. Onboarding isn't over until offboarding begins. Never stop inspiring and enabling your new employee to pursue mastery and better results faster.

Help Your New Employees Adjust

Inevitably, there will be surprises. Help your new employee see them coming. Help him or her figure out if the surprises are major or minor with a temporary or enduring impact.[3] Guide him or her to downplay responses to minor surprises with temporary impact, evolve adjustments to minor surprises with enduring impact, manage major surprises with temporary impact, and hit a restart button and perhaps even invest in reboarding when faced with major surprises with enduring impact.

You should adjust and improve, too. Evaluate your performance in onboarding your new employees, and plan to do an even better job with your next onboarding.

Lead

Onboarding is one of the acid tests of leadership. If you follow the prescriptions in this book and stay focused on inspiring and enabling others to do their absolute best, together to realize a meaningful and rewarding shared purpose, then those others will happily follow you.

Organization-Wide Transformation

T he main body of this book is designed to help one manager onboard one new employee. This appendix recaps our ideas about how to make an organization-wide transformation to more effective onboarding that gets all new employees up to speed in half the time and strengthens an organization's culture.

When you implement all of the ideas presented in the chapter "Master Class" callouts, and more and more hiring managers implement Total Onboarding Programs in the same organization, successes compound. Performance results and standards rise across the organization, which evolves the culture in a very positive way.

Let's recap the Master Class ideas:

Look at overall organizational messaging on an annual basis as part of your normal succession planning and talent management processes. Get all employees aligned around the overall messaging that they will cascade down in their own Total Onboarding Programs. This annual messaging review increases consistency across individual messages and gives everyone a chance for deliberate practice to build knowledge and skills in crafting and critiquing messaging.

Embed onboarding in your normal succession planning and talent management processes. As you examine what roles you need to fill in the future, get everyone aligned around hypothetical Total Onboarding Programs for those positions to give your managers a head start on filling those positions when the time is right and give everyone a chance for deliberate practice to build knowledge and skills in crafting and critiquing Total Onboarding Programs and recruiting briefs.

Create a culture of continuous sourcing. Direct and train your managers to always be on the lookout for potentially good additions to their teams, internally and externally. Managers will improve their sourcing knowledge and skills and build a very strong pool of potential candidates for future opportunities.

Set aside one day each month for interviews. All appropriate managers should keep these days open whenever possible. A fixed, monthly interview day makes it easier to schedule candidates for interviews and gives managers an opportunity for regular, deliberate interview practice. The regularly occurring interview day also signals the importance of your Total Onboarding Program to the organization and potential employees.

Make training on strategic selling mandatory for *all* managers. Everybody can benefit from deliberate practice in strategic selling because everybody can do a better job of understanding others' needs, figuring out how to solve others' problems, and communicating those solutions to the people involved.

Create an onboarding plan review board to provide managers and their new employees input on personal onboarding plans. A review board supports cross-fertilization of the best ideas in personal onboarding plans while deepening the knowledge and skills of the onboarding managers and the members of the review board.

Run announcement cascade plans past the onboarding plan review board to further cross-fertilization of the best ideas in announcement cascades while deepening the knowledge and skills of the onboarding managers and the members of the review board.

Systematize accommodation so you don't have to reinvent it every time. Accommodation is one of those areas where being "good enough" cost effectively is all you need. Spend your time creating superior knowledge and skills in other areas.

Create a prototypical day one agenda that you can adjust to fit each new employee's situation. Continually evaluate and evolve that prototypical agenda as you learn.

Set aside one day each month for group orientations. This will allow you to make the orientations a bigger deal with more regular senior management involvement. Monthly orientation also facilitates creation of onboarding cohorts.

Create a newcomers' club with executive sponsors. A newcomers' club helps new employees learn from each other's and executive sponsors' experiences and connections. It gives executives opportunities to get informal feedback from people with fresh eyes, signal the importance of onboarding, reinforce their vision and values, and deliberately practice helping people at all levels assimilate into the organization.

Create a stable of internal and external mentors, coaches, and transition accelerators ready to help accelerate groups. To build expertise and institutionalize knowledge, have periodic meetings of the people in your stable to share learning about accelerating transitions in your organization.

Additionally, have a system to track and measure progress. Think about looking at these dimensions:

Scorecard—Total Onboarding Program Metrics

- Retention rate of new employees (within first 18 months or year of employment)
- New employee engagement (through something like Gallup's system)
- Employee satisfaction with the onboarding process (through survey below)
- Competitive advantages created by the Total Onboarding Program (perhaps with a submeasure of retention like valued losses)
- Onboarding program as positive employment differentiation in the marketplace (perhaps with a measure of response to recruiting ads, competitive salaries)
- New employee alignment with business goals (perhaps with performance ratings)

New Employee Fresh Eyes Survey

Use this simple survey to capture new employee appraisals and feelings while they are fresh. If possible, human resources should conduct the survey and give new employees the option of allowing their hiring managers to see their responses or submitting responses anonymously to the pooled survey results that human resources maintains, tabulates, and disseminates once or twice a year.

Conduct the survey four times, at the end of your new employee's:

- First week
- First month

- Second month
- First 100 days

Survey

New employees are one of the best sources of knowledge and innovation. We want to know what you've learned about our organization and what you think we can improve.

1. How likely is it that you would recommend [Company X] to a friend or colleague?[1]

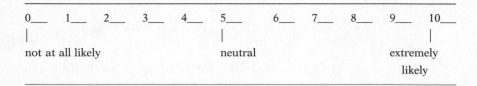

0___ 1___ 2___ 3___ 4___ 5___   6___ 7___ 8___ 9___ 10___

not at all likely   neutral   extremely
                                                            likely

2. Please tell us about your (first week/first month/first couple of months/first 100 days).
   a. What about your onboarding has gone particularly well?
   b. What about your onboarding could be improved or changed for you or others?
3. Please describe in your own words the three *most important* things you do in your job.
4. Name the three *most enjoyable* aspects of your job.
5. Name the three *least enjoyable* aspects of your job.
6. Please share your thoughts about possible improvements to the way we run our business.

Sourcing Candidates on the Web

We wish we could offer a definitive list of Web recruiting resources. But the world changes too quickly. Instead, here are broad suggestions to get you started:

1. *Find and engage thought leaders.* People with expertise showcase their knowledge on the Web by blogging, commenting on blogs, and answering questions posted by others:
   a. Find the thought leaders with web searches.
      i. Google
      ii. About ("About.com is an online neighborhood of hundreds of helpful experts, eager to share their wealth of knowledge with visitors.").
      iii. Technorati ("founded to help bloggers succeed by collecting, highlighting, and distributing the online global conversation. As the leading blog search engine and most comprehensive source of information on the blogosphere, we index more than 1.5 million new blog posts in real time and introduce millions of readers to blog and social media content.")
      iv. Addictomatic ("Addictomatic searches the best live sites on the Web for the latest news, blog posts, videos, and images. It's the perfect tool to keep up with the hottest topics, perform ego searches, and feed your addiction for what's up, what's now, or what other people are feeding on.")
   b. Comment on thought leader blog postings to start the conversation.
   c. Attract the thought leaders you seek by posting questions on Q&A pages.
      i. LinkedIn

ii. Amazon ("Amazon.com has millions of customers who are passionate about a diverse range of hobbies and interests. You can share your experiences and enthusiasm for your favorite topics with this community of like-minded [and sometimes different-minded] people. Customer Community pages provide a home on Amazon.com for thousands of topics, with new ones being added every day by our customers. From the Action community to the Zombies community and everything in between, we probably have you covered.")

iii. Yahoo (answers.yahoo.com)

2. *Network.* Recruiting is no longer about finding and screening prospects. It is now about prospecting, qualifying, nurturing, and converting leads. Networks constitute a big part of the sales funnel:

a. LinkedIn

b. Yahoo! 360

c. Facebook

d. MySpace

e. Career Networks

i. www.theladders.com

"We are the world's largest community catering exclusively to the $100k+ job market. TheLadders.com offers online job search resources and content for the $100k+ job seekers and recruiters. Our specialized job search engines are an invaluable asset to top-earning job seekers in Sales, Marketing, Finance, Human Resources, Law, Technology, Operations, and all other $100k+ fields."

ii. www.execunet.com

"Pinpoint active and hard-to-find passive candidates, connect with high-quality business leaders, and stay informed of best practices and market trends."

3. *Post job openings.* Begin your online search by posting your job opening on a couple of big, general job boards and 3 to 5 niche sites. Include niches sites that cover your opening's industry, geography, and profession:

a. The Big Boards

i. RealMatch ("Our mission is to create a platform that provides employers and job seekers a better way to connect . . . a technology that allows employers and job seekers to specifically define themselves, their needs, and their preferences.")

ii. Jobfox ("We provide what no other job site can—Introductions between highly matched job seeking professionals and employers.")

iii. CareerBuilder ("Our mission is to be the global leader in online recruitment advertising by being an employee-driven, customer-focused organization that provides the best rate of return to our stakeholders.")

iv. Monster ("As the migration to the Internet continues, over 75 million of Monster's visitors have established personalized accounts that take advantage of our wide breadth of services, including our global resume database or proprietary job search agent technology, that enables them to better manage their careers. Monster Worldwide is consistently ranked among the top 20 most visited sites on the Internet.")

v. Craigslist ("Local classifieds and forums for more than 550 cities in over 50 countries worldwide—community moderated, and largely free.")

vi. Yahoo! HotJobs ("Yahoo! HotJobs' tools and advice put job seekers in control of their careers and make it easier and more cost-effective for employers and staffing firms to find qualified candidates. In addition to its popular consumer job board, Yahoo! HotJobs provides employers, recruiters, and staffing agencies with progressive recruiting solutions.")

4. *Explore niche sites.* Wikipedia is a good place to source niche job boards and social networking sites.

5. *Watch the aggregators.* Make sure the big job-posting aggregators pick up your postings. These are search engines that crawl job boards and corporate web sites for listings based on the keywords you select:

a. Indeed

b. JobSniper

c. SimplyHired

NOTES

Chapter 1: Understand the Organization-Wide Benefits of a Total Onboarding Program: An Executive Summary

1. This is the first of several quotes from managers around the world who agreed to let us use their words just so long as we preserved their confidentiality.
2. Kevin Martin, presentation to the Human Capital Institute, Washington, DC, April 16, 2008. Aberdeen's group 2007 study indicated that 86 percent of employees make a decision to stay or leave the firm in their first six months or less.
3. Brad Smart, *Topgrading* (Upper Saddle River, NJ: Prentice Hall, 1999).
4. As quoted by Brooke Masters in "Rise of a Headhunter" *Financial Times*, March 30, 2009.
5. PrimeGenesis has reduced the failure rate fourfold for new leader's it's helped from 40 percent to 10 percent.
6. See George B. Bradt, Jayme A. Check, and Jorge E. Pedraza, *The New Leader's 100-Day Action Plan*, 2nd ed. (Hoboken, NJ: John Wiley & Sons, 2009); or www.primegenesis.com for more on these building blocks.

Chapter 2: Clarify Your Destination Messages to the Candidate and the Organization

1. This story, like all the stories in this book, is true. We've changed the details to preserve confidentiality, but core events in each story happened.
2. As director of the Human Capital Institute's Talent Leadership Community, Andy Kriz is responsible for researching, synthesizing, and presenting thought-provoking ideas and topics critical to the success of business leaders and organizations to meet their current and future leadership challenges. Andy's comments here are taken from a series of conversation between him and George Bradt throughout 2008 and from his HCI Talent Leadership blog.
3. This tool, and most of the tools in this book are downloadable from www.onboarding-tools.com.

Chapter 3: Craft Your Time Line, Write a Recruiting Brief, and Align Your Stakeholders

1. Marcus Buckingham and Don Clifton, *Now Discover Your Strengths* (New York: Free Press, 2001); Geoff Colvin, *Talent Is Overrated* (New York:

Penguin, 2008). Buckingham and Clifton argue that talent is innate. Geoff Colvin argues talent is irrelevant.

Chapter 4: Create a Powerful Slate of Potential Candidates

1. Bill Berman, PhD, a clinical and consulting psychologist, has worked with a number of public and private companies. He is co-author of 3 books and over 50 articles on a variety of psychology and business topics. He is a fellow of the American Psychological Association and is board-certified by the American Board of Professional Psychology and has taught at Cornell Medical College and Fordham University. Bill wrote this piece for this publication.
2. These generation descriptions are drawn from work by Tamara Erickson and others. See Tamara's "Guest Expert" block in chapter 10 of this book.
3. David Lord founded Executive Search Information Services in 1995 in response to requests from corporations for better information about executive recruiters and best practices in working with them. Since then, he has helped more than 100 Fortune 500 corporations improve executive search effectiveness.
4. David Lord, "Executive Talent: A Global Perspective," remarks at the Search-Consult conference, Frankfurt, Germany, October 21, 2008.
5. With Sheila's leadership responsibilities as president and chief executive officer of Sheila Greco Associates, LLC and her active role in the overall growth and success of the company, she places her broad-based skills and experience at the disposal of clients, candidates, and colleagues alike. As an entrepreneur, she has gained extensive experience in human resources to include, research, recruiting, and competitive intelligence. As a strategic results-oriented leader, Sheila has a proven track record of building long-term and solid relationships with clients and candidates.
6. This is an excerpt from Sheila Greco's December 16, 2008, interview with RecruitingBlogs.com.

Chapter 5: Evaluate Candidates Against the Recruiting Brief while Pre-Selling and Pre-Boarding

1. Bill Noll has owned and operated Noll Human Resource Services for 32 years. Prior to that, he was an architect and user of selection services provided by Selection Research (now Gallup). He changed professions and set out on a mission to help growth-oriented companies pick and develop talented and capable people. Noll and his team do about 80 percent of their work in predictive analysis for leaders wanting to make a final decision from sourced candidates. About 20 percent of their work is assisting in developmental programs for staff based on their revealed talent.

2. Marcus Buckingham and Don Clifton, *Now Discover Your Strengths* (New York: Free Press, 2001).
3. Oren Trask does not actually exist. He's a character in *Working Girl*, directed by Kevin Wade (Los Angeles: Twentieth Century-Fox, 1986). His thinking is too powerful to leave out just because he isn't real.
4. Geoffrey Smart is Chairman and CEO of ghSMART & Co., a management assessment and coaching firm.
5. Geoff Smart and Randy Street, *Who* (New York: Ballantine Books, 2008); and conversations with George Bradt, 2005.

Chapter 6: Make the Right Offer, and Close the Right Sale the Right Way

1. Bill Epifanio is managing partner with Stratis, a premier Human Capital Consulting and Search firm specializing in clean technology, renewable energy, and financial technology sectors.

Chapter 8: Manage the Announcement to Set Your New Employee Up for Success

1. Significant parts of this are lifted or adapted from George B. Bradt, Jayme A. Check, and Jorge E. Pedraza's *The New Leader's 100-Day Action Plan*, 2nd ed. (Hoboken, NJ: John Wiley & Sons, 2009), as they should be, because new employees and their bosses' messages should overlap.
2. This thinking is derived from Teresa M. Amabile and Steven J. Kramer, "Inner Work Life," *Harvard Business Review* (May 2007): 72–83.
3. Jean Brown wrote this for this publication. A principal at MacKenzie Brown, Jean coaches senior executives to help them enhance their leadership presence and communicate with impact. She brings together business experience with eight years as a professional actress, singer, and dancer/choreographer.

Chapter 9: Do What It Takes to Make Your New Employee Ready, Eager, and Able to Do Real Work on Day One

1. Faye Hansen, "Onboarding for Greater Engagement," *Workforce Management*, October 2008.
2. George Selix, PhD, is a senior director, partner and Employee Learning at Sun Microsystems. These ideas were shared in an interview with George Bradt, November 5, 2008.
3. Thomas. H. Holmes and Richard H. Rahe, "The Social Readjustment Rating Scale," *Journal of Psychosomatic Research* 11, no. 2 (1967): 213–218.

Chapter 10: Make Positive First Impressions Both Ways

1. Kevin Martin, presentation to Human Capital Institute, April 16, 2008. Aberdeen's group 2007 study indicated that 86 percent of employees make a decision to stay or leave the firm in their first six months or less.
2. David Lee is the founder of HumanNature@Work and a consultant, speaker, and author of dozens of articles on employee performance.
3. These ideas are drawn from David Lee, "Onboarding That Welcomes and Inspires: What Do Ritz Carlton, Southwest Airlines, and Texas Roadhouse 'Get' That Other Employers Don't?" *ERE.net*, April 10, 2008; and conversations with David throughout 2008.

Chapter 11: Speed Development of Important Working Relationships

1. Lyn Heward and John Bacon, *Cirque du Soleil® the Spark: Igniting the Creative Fire That Lives within Us* (New York: Random House, 2006).
2. Large parts of this section were lifted from George B. Bradt, Jayme A. Check, and Jorge E. Pedraza's *The New Leader's 100-Day Action Plan*, 2nd ed. (Hoboken, NJ: John Wiley & Sons, 2009), since they are equally applicable here. (Probably means you should get a discount on that book when you buy it.)
3. See Edgar Schein, *Organizational Culture and Leadership* (San Francisco: Jossey-Bass, 1985).
4. Chang Klarissa, Kate Ehrlich, and David Millen, "Getting on Board: A Social Network Analysis of the Transformation of New Hires into Full-Time Employees," paper presented at the meeting of Computer-Supported Cooperative Work, Workshop on Social Networks, Chicago, November 6–10, 2004.
5. Robert Cross, "The Intersection of Social Networks and Talent Management," presented to the Human Capital Institute, June 9, 2008.
6. Robert Cross, From an interview with George Bradt, December 11, 2008.
7. Maude Divittis is the founder of ExecOnBoard LLC, an organization that successfully supports accelerated workplace performance during transition. She has supplemented her invaluable practical experience at Mars and MTV (SVP of Learning and Development) with in-depth research into onboarding as part of her doctoral work at Columbia.
8. Maude's ideas are compiled from her presentation "Identifying Solutions for Effective Individual + Team Onboarding" to the American Society for Training and Development International Conference Exposition, San Diego, CA, June 1, 2008, and a series of conversations between her and George Bradt 2005–2008.

9. Robert Cross, "Relational Onboarding: How Social Networking Accelerates New Hires into Star Performers," Human Capital Institute webcast, December 6, 2007.
10. From Keith Rollag, Salvatore Parise, and Rob Cross, "Getting New Hires Up to Speed Quickly," *MIT Sloan Management Review* 46, no. 2 (2005).
11. Robert Cross, from an interview with George Bradt, December 11, 2008.
12. This is derived from Tamara Erickson's talk "Demography Is Destiny: Four Generations in the Workforce Today and Affects on Onboarding" at the International Quality and Productivity Center's conference on onboarding, San Jose, CA, June 17, 2008.

Chapter 12: Provide Resources, Support, and Follow-Through

1. See George B. Bradt, Jayme A. Check, and Jorge E. Pedraza's *The New Leader's 100-Day Action Plan*, 2nd ed. (Hoboken, NJ: John Wiley & Sons, 2009) or www.primegenesis.com for more on these building blocks. Indeed, large portions of this chapter are lifted and/or adapted from that book and work.
2. Fred Reichheld, "The One Number You Need to Grow," *Harvard Business Review*, December 2003.
3. There's more on this in Bradt, Check, and Pedraza's *The New Leader's 100-Day Action Plan*.

Appendix 1: Organization-Wide Transformation

1. Fred Reichheld, "The One Number You Need to Grow," *Harvard Business Review*, December 2003.

As much as possible, we tried to avoid jargon or consultantspeak. When we felt compelled to use words with special meanings in the context of onboarding, we included them here.

Accelerate: Help new employees and their teams be more productive faster.

Accommodate: Give new team members the tools they need to do work.

Acquire: In this case, identifying, recruiting, selecting, and getting people to agree to joining the team—one of the early steps in a total onboarding program.

Alignment: Getting everyone going in the same direction, positioned relative to each other so that together they achieve the desired results.

Assimilate: Help new employees join with others so that they can work together.

Blog: A Web log, online compilation of thoughts, stories, comments, and so on.

Brokers: A person acting as an agent for someone else or an intermediary.

Buddy: Someone looking out for someone else—particularly useful in assimilating a new employee.

Coach: Someone to teach, train, and guide a new employee (or anyone else).

Cohort: Group of people with something in common (like starting new jobs at the same time).

Connectors: People who connect others to helpful people or resources.

EASE: Encourage, Align, Solve, and End.

Employment brand: How your organization is perceived by current, future, and past employees.

Engagement: Being actively involved in something. (In this case, caring about your job and organization.)

Flipping: An online-research tactic that allows recruiters to pinpoint candidates by uncovering personal Web sites linked to competitor employee directories, organizational charts, and membership in professional organizations.

Formal/informal network: People working together. The formal network is what's published in organization charts, charters, and the like. Often the informal network is the way things really happen.

Fresh eyes: Someone looking at something for the first time without the biases or filters of having seen the same thing over and over again.

Fuzzy front end: The time between accepting a job and day one.

Gallup: A research company in Nebraska that has done a lot of work on organizational behaviors.

High-performing team: A group of people working interdependently to deliver a common goal at a high level of performance.

Human capital: People. The term is designed to signal the importance of investing in people.

Mentor: An informal coach.

NewJobPrep.com: An online, self-managed tool for creating a new job plan. Created by George Bradt and Mary Vonnegut, based on the ideas in *The New Leader's 100-Day Action Plan*.

New manager assimilation session: Originally created by Lynn Ulrich of the Jarvis institute and deployed in great depth at GE—a facilitated session in which new managers answer a group's questions in an open forum. It is described in *The New Leader's 100-Day Action Plan*.

Onboarding: Efforts to acquire, accommodate, assimilate, and accelerate new team members, whether they come from outside or inside the organization.

Onboarding portal: Software designed to facilitate new employee accommodation, generally focused on employment forms and tools.

Peripherals: Things that are less crucial to the task.

PrimeGenesis: Leading onboarding and transition acceleration firm. The authors, George Bradt and Mary Vonnegut are partners in PrimeGenesis.

Shadow network: Another phrase for the informal network. Often the way information and resources really flow in an organization.

Spiders and snakes: Internet-recruiting programs that scan job boards for resumes of attractive candidates.

Stakeholders: People with direct interest, involvement, or a stake in an organization or individual's pursuits.

STAR interviewing: Situation, Task Action, and Results. Great way to get people to provide examples of strengths.

Talent leadership: Efforts to make an organization more ADEPT— Acquire, Develop, Encourage, Plan, and Transition talent.

TOP: Total Onboarding Program—comprehensive approach to onboarding from acquiring, accommodating, assimilating, through to accelerating.

Touchstone: Person who can tell the truth to the new employee. Touchstone was the fool in Shakespeare's "As You Like It" and one of the few people who could tell the truth.

Transition acceleration: Helping new employees and their teams deliver better results faster.

Wiki: A piece of server software that allows users to freely create and edit Web page content.

REFERENCES

Amabile, Teresa M., and Steven J. Kramer. "Inner Work Life." *Harvard Business Review*, May 2007:72–83.

Ben-Shahar, Tal. *Happier*. New York: McGraw-Hill, 2007.

Bradt, George B., Jayme A. Check, and Jorge E. Pedraza. *The New Leader's 100-Day Action Plan*. 2nd ed. Hoboken, NJ: John Wiley & Sons, 2009.

Brown, Jean. Written contribution for this publication, 2008; and series of conversations with George Bradt 2005–2008.

Buckingham, Marcus, and Don Clifton. *Now Discover Your Strengths*. New York: Free Press, 2001.

Colvin, Geoff. *Talent Is Overrated*. New York, NY: Penguin, 2008.

Chang, Klarissa, Kate Ehrlich, and David Millen. "Getting on Board: A Social Network Analysis of the Transformation of New Hires into Full-Time Employees." Paper presented at the meeting of Computer-Supported Cooperative Work, Workshop on Social Networks, Chicago, November 6–10, 2004.

Cross, Robert. "The Intersection of Social Networks and Talent Management" (Webcast). Washington, DC: Human Capital Institute, June 9, 2008; and conversations with George Bradt during 2008.

Cross, Robert. "Relational Onboarding: How Social Networking Accelerates New Hires into Star Performers" (Webcast). Washington, DC: Human Capital Institute, December 6, 2007.

Divittis, Maude. "Identifying Solutions for Effective Individual + Team Onboarding" presentation to the American Society for Training and Development International Conference Exposition, San Diego, CA, June 1, 2008; and series of conversations with George Bradt 2005–2008.

Erickson, Tamara. "Demography Is Destiny: Four Generations in the Workforce Today and Affects on Onboarding" presentation at the International Quality and Productivity Center's conference on onboarding, San Jose, CA, June 17, 2008.

Ericsson, K. Anders, Ralf Th. Krampe, and Clemens Tesch-Romer. "The Role of Deliberate Practice in the Acquisition of Expert Performance." *Psychological Review* 100(3):363–406.

Greco, Sheila. Interview with RecruitingBlogs.com, December 16, 2008.

Guber, Peter. "The Four Truths of the Storyteller." *Harvard Business Review*, December 2007: 52–59.

Hansen, Faye. "Onboarding for Greater Engagement." *Workforce Management*, October 2008.

Heward, Lyn, and John Bacon. *Cirque du Soleil® the Spark: Igniting the Creative Fire That Lives within Us*. New York: Random House, 2006.

Kriz, Andy. [Various entries]. *Human Capital Institute Blog*, 2008; http://www. humancapitalinstitute.org/hci/research_blogs_blog.guid;jsessionid= C1BBCBCBB69CFC58E1123C719EF2A5C1?_blogID=327; and series of conversations with George Bradt during 2008.

Lee, David. "Onboarding That Welcomes and Inspires: What Do Ritz Carlton, Southwest Airlines, and Texas Roadhouse 'Get' That Other Employers Don't?" *ERE.net*, April 10, 2008; and conversations with George Bradt throughout 2008.

Lord, David. "Executive Talent: A Global Perspective." Remarks to the Search-Consult Conference, Frankfurt, Germany, October 21, 2008.

Martin, Kevin. *"Set the Stage for Performance Deliverables through Onboarding"* Webcast. Washington, DC: Human Capital Institute, April 16, 2008.

McDermott, Meaghan. Article on Jean-Claude Brizard. *Rochester Democrat and Chronicle*, January 2, 2008.

Noll, Bill. Written contribution for this publication and conversations with George Bradt, 2008.

Rollag, Keith, Salvatore Parise, and Rob Cross. "Getting New Hires Up to Speed Quickly." *MIT Sloan Management Review*, 46(2).

Schein, Edgar. *Organizational Culture and Leadership*. San Francisco: Jossey-Bass,1985.

Smart, Brad. *Topgrading*. Upper Saddle River, NJ: Prentice Hall,1999.

Smart, Geoff.Conversations with George Bradt in 2005.

Smart Geoff, and Randy Street. *Who*. New York: Ballantine Books, 2008.

Sperling, Michael B., and William H. Berman, eds. *Attachment in Adults*. New York: Guilford Press, 1994.

Working Girl. Directed by Kevin, Wade. Los Angeles: Twentieth Century-Fox, 1986.

Bill Berman, PhD, a clinical and consulting psychologist and partner in PrimeGenesis, is co-author of 3 books and over 50 articles on a variety of psychology and business topics. He is a fellow of the American Psychological Association and is board-certified by the American Board of Professional Psychology and has taught at Cornell Medical College and Fordham University. Bill can be found in chapter 4 of this book and at bberman @primegenesis.com.

Jean Brown, a principal at MacKenzie Brown, coaches senior executives to help them enhance their leadership presence and communicate with impact. She brings together business experience with eight years as a professional actress, singer, and dancer/ choreographer. Jean can be found in chapter 8 of this book and at jbrown@mackenziebrown.biz.

Rob Cross of the University of Virginia has been studying social networks for a decade. He and his Network Roundtable have discovered that high performers have noninsular networks. They reach out up, across, and down in a number of important ways. Rob can be found in chapter 11 of this book and at robcross @virginia.edu.

Maude Divittis is the founder of ExecOnBoard LLC, an organization that successfully supports accelerated workplace performance during transition. She has supplemented her invaluable practical experience at Mars and MTV (SVP of Learning and Development) with in-depth research into onboarding as part of her doctoral work at Columbia. Maude can be found in chapter 11 of this book and at maude@execonboard.com.

Bill Epifanio is managing partner with Stratis, a premier Human Capital Consulting and Search firm where he serves technology and financial services clients seeking to fully capitalize on the strategic capabilities of technology, recruiting leadership to implement innovative processes and services while negotiating integration issues. Bill can be found in chapter 6 of this book and at bill@stratis1.com.

Tamara Erickson of the Concours Institute talks about differences in onboarding across four generational cohorts: Traditionalists (born 1928–1945), Baby Boomers (1946–1960), Generation Xers (1961–1980), and Generation Yers (1981–2000). Tammy can be found in chapter 11 of this book and at tammy@tammyerickson.com.

Sheila Greco is president and chief executive officer of Sheila Greco Associates, LLC and has extensive experience in human resources that includes research, recruiting, and competitive intelligence. Sheila can be found in chapter 4 of this book and at sgreco@sheilagreco.com.

Andy Kriz, director of the Talent Leadership Community at the Human Capital Institute is a big proponent of talent as an investment. Andy can be found in chapter 2 of this book and at andrew@krisresearch.com.

David Lee is the founder of HumanNature@Work and a consultant, speaker, and author of dozens of articles on employee performance. David can be found in chapter 10 of this book and at info@humannatureatwork.com.

David Lord founded Executive Search Information Systems in 1995, in response to requests from corporations for better information about executive recruiters and best practices in working with them. David can be found in chapter 4 of this book and at david@davidlord.com.

Bill Noll owns and runs Noll Human Resource Services. He started his career as an architect and then moved on to Gallup when he decided it was much more interesting to build people than to build buildings. Bill can be found in chapter 5 of this book and at bill@noll.com.

George Selix, PhD is the senior director for Partner and Employee Learning at Sun Microsystems, with responsibility for training 33,000 employees and over 80,000 partners. His responsibilities include new employee onboarding, compliance training, leadership development, skills acquisition, and professional development.

George can be found in chapter 9 of this book and at gselixl @carolina.rr.com.

Geoffrey Smart is chairman and CEO of ghSMART, the management assessment firm for CEOs and investors, which he founded in 1995. Geoff can be found in chapter 5 of this book and at ghsmart@ghsmart.com.

Oren Trask was CEO of media conglomerate Trask Industries and was particularly gifted in choosing great people. Oren can be found in chapter 5 of this book.

George Bradt has a unique perspective on helping people move into new roles. After Harvard and Wharton, George spent two decades in sales, marketing, and general management around the world at companies including Unilever, Procter & Gamble, Coca-Cola, and then J.D. Power and Associates as chief executive of its Power Information Network spin-off. Now he is managing director of PrimeGenesis, the executive onboarding and transition acceleration group he founded in 2002. George can be reached at gbradt@primegenesis.com.

Mary Vonnegut, former president of Gumps Catalog and SVP marketing at Hanover Direct, has spent most of her career in direct and database marketing as a senior line manager and independent consultant. Mary has worked with diverse product categories from high-end jewelry to moving-and-storage franchise services in both entrepreneurial and corporate environments. She has launched new businesses, built marketing departments from the ground up and crafted growth strategies. Now she is a partner in PrimeGenesis. Mary earned a BA from Middlebury and an MBA from Harvard. Mary can be reached at mvonnegut@prime genesis.com.